RICHMOND AT WAR
1939-1945

by

Simon Fowler

The Richmond Local History Society

Text © The Richmond Local History Society 2015

ISBN 978-0-9550717.8.2

Illustrations

Pages 9,10,20,25,28,30,35-6,38
Courtesy Richmond upon Thames Local Studies Library and
Archive

Pages 12,14,43,45,54,58,63,66,83,85,87
Courtesy the Museum of Richmond

Page 71
Courtesy the Hearsum Collection

Page 46
Courtesy Cuthbert Orde, Pilots of Fighter Command
(Harrap, 1942)

Page 76
Courtesy the Imperial War Museum: image H1257

Front Cover: Peldon Avenue 1940
Courtesy Richmond upon Thames Local Studies Library and
Archive

Back cover: 'Richmond Hill on VE Day' by Mary Kent Harrison
Courtesy Stephen Kent Harrison

Printed in Great Britain by Doppler Press,
26 Eldon Way, Hockley, Essex SS5 4AD

Contents

PREFACE

This is a short account of the years of the Second World War in Richmond and how it affected local people. It concentrates largely on the air raids on the town and the effect they had. This is not to dismiss other aspects of the war in Richmond, which profoundly affected every resident whether they were six or sixty. However, the Blitz and the V1 attacks had the greatest immediate impact on local people and the local townscape.

The raids put civilians on the frontline and made the home front the battlefront across much of Britain, in a way that had never happened before and we hope will never happen again. As a result, the records and the memories of the raids are fuller than for any other aspects of the war. In addition, the raids and the need to prepare for them influenced life in a multitude of ways – from walks in Richmond Park and the activities of the Home Guard to school examinations and eating out.

What comes through are the remarkable bravery and stoicism of the people of Richmond, who before the war could never have imagined the events of 1940 and 1941, let alone the V1 self-propelled rockets that were straight out of science fiction. As one local resident pointed out, 'My house was bombed, but we carried on. We had to really – we were all in the same boat.'[i]

That is not to say that people maintained the stiff upper lip of wartime film and propaganda. Some people were clearly traumatised by their experiences, while many others just complained about the lack of sleep caused by spending nights shivering in damp shelters. Yet remarkably there seems to have been no protests, nor even mutterings against the war, although there was plenty of grumbling. To a remarkable degree the people of Richmond stood solidly behind Winston Churchill.

This volume is the latest in a series being published by the borough's local history societies. There was no planning in this, just a coincidence. Each book takes a different approach, but between them they give the reader an idea of what the war was like right across Richmond upon Thames. They are listed under Sources on page 92.

Simon Fowler, Kew, August 2015

---

[i]   Museum of Richmond, *Catalogue for Richmond at War: the Civilian Experience 1939-45* (Museum of Richmond, 1992), p2.

4

CHAPTER 1 – *Richmond before WW2*

In September 1939 Richmond was an affluent suburb on the edge of London. By Richmond we mean the town of Richmond, which was the largest part of the Borough of Richmond (Surrey). The Borough also included Kew, Ham and Petersham as well as much of Richmond Park. To the east of Clifford Avenue was Barnes Urban District Council, and across the Thames lay Twickenham and the county of Middlesex. In turn Richmond was divided into ten wards of which six were in the town.

Richmond itself was part of the county of Surrey. The County Council was responsible for education, roads and various other matters. However, responsibility for Air Raid Precautions and many other concerns relating to the preparation for war had been delegated to the Borough Council, although in this they would be largely directed by the Home Office and later by the Ministry of Home Security in Whitehall. These details may seem arcane today, but they were not to the politicians and administrators seventy-five years ago. The small size of the Borough helped encourage local pride, which may be lacking today, but certainly came to the fore during the war.

The Borough Council consisted of 29 councillors, 25 of whom were Independents. The others were four Labour men, one of whom, H A Leon, would be mayor between 1940 and 1941. In addition there were ten aldermen, who were mostly former councillors. From among these numbers a mayor was elected annually to represent Richmond and its citizens. It was a duty that was taken very seriously.

Party politics were deplored by the Conservatives, and Richmond was a safe Conservative area. During the War the local MP, George Harvie-Watt, would serve as Principal Parliamentary Secretary to Winston Churchill, keeping the Prime Minister in touch with the views of MPs.

In the late 1930s Richmond had yet to be absorbed into London. The authors of *Towards a Plan for Richmond*, published in 1945, which aimed to produce a post-war plan for the borough, described the area thus:

> In spite of the outward sprawl from London Richmond has maintained a real character and individuality and withstood in large measure the ravages of indiscriminate development... Certain areas, characterised by dignified architecture, depict an air

of culture and in the by-ways are to be found many places of great interest and charm...Yet many defects and inadequacies remain and are all too often apparent.[i]

The writer Arthur Mee noted in 1938, 'Although it is almost London, [Richmond] seems to take delight in eluding the bands of brick that would enclose it.' Even so, between the wars the few remaining market gardens towards Sheen and Mortlake were covered with housing, physically joining the town with the metropolis, and blocks of flats were built at the top of Richmond Hill and along Sheen Road. There were also small pockets of social deprivation; the 1945 Plan identified twelve 'congested and ill-planned areas', and recommended that they should be redeveloped. In 1939 these housed 8000 inhabitants.[ii]

For most people, Richmond was an agreeable place to live in, with good connections to central London, both by the Underground and by the Southern Railway to Waterloo, as well as having many good shops, schools and entertainments. There were also a number of light industries, notably the British Legion Poppy Factory, which employed disabled ex-servicemen. Other big local employers were Chrysler Motors and Courtaulds (who made artificial fabrics) in Kew and the Hawker Aircraft Factory in Ham.

The area was a favourite place for tourists, who thronged the riverside and Richmond Hill or walked across Richmond Park on fine days. Although his book was not published until 1949 William Palmer surely had pre-war Richmond in mind when he wrote:
> For parks, shrubberies, lawns and flower gardens, Richmond sets a high standard and is not easily equalled, let alone excelled. A great variety of pleasures and amusements, quite apart from those on the river, are offered and the place is celebrated for fine music, both outdoors and in.[iii]

The census and other records give some idea of who lived in Richmond. In 1931 almost exactly 38,000 people lived in the Borough. The number had fallen slightly to 34,100 by September 1939 (of whom 20,000 lived in the town of Richmond itself). The decline may be explained by the numbers of men who had already been called up. [iv]

Residents were somewhat older and wealthier than the national average. Half the population was between the ages of 25 and 55. There were rather more women than men: in part this may reflect the demographic changes wrought by the First World War.

Many men were employed in white-collar trades, particularly in 'Commerce and Trade' and as 'Clerks and Draughtsmen'. Rather fewer women worked, and those who did were overwhelmingly 'personal servants', employed to clean and cook in the houses of the middle-class residents.

Planning for War

Preparations for war began, throughout the country, almost four years before war was formally declared. As early as 1932 Stanley Baldwin, then leader of the Conservative Party, had issued this warning:

> I think it is well for the man in the street to realise that there is no power on earth that can prevent him from being bombed. Whatever people may tell him, the bomber will always get through.[v]

Graphic evidence supporting Baldwin's message came in newsreels showing horrific damage inflicted on towns and cities by German and Italian bombers during the Spanish Civil War (1936-39). The experiences in Spain had a profound impact on Civil Defence planning in Britain. It was assumed, without questioning, that terrible devastation would come from the skies in the form both of high explosive bombs and gas attacks. All the authorities could do was to minimise the devastation as best they could.

The first meeting of Richmond Council's Air Raid Precautions Sub-Committee took place as early as February 1936. It was not well attended. Members discussed completing a questionnaire circulated by Surrey County Council. However, as war came ever closer so did the importance of this sub-committee increase. Renamed first as the Emergency Committee, then as the Civil Defence Committee, it appointed staff, recruited volunteers, built shelters and planned in minute detail the response to air raids.

As well as dealing with the threat from conventional bombs they had to prepare for gas attacks. Richmond's Draft ARP Plan of October 1936 suggested that there should be a gas decontamination area for men in the first-class areas at the Public Baths in Parkshot, which included a swimming bath, dressing cubicles, clubroom and dressing room. Women were to have the second-class side of the baths.

Fortunately in the event neither side used gas.[vi]

Inevitably there were problems. Perhaps the greatest was the lack of volunteers. The 1936 plan called for 1854 volunteers – nearly five per cent of the Borough's population. At the beginning of 1937 the Council modified the target to 600 men and 400 women. In February 1938 the Mayor wrote to all ratepayers appealing for volunteers:

> It is imperative for our own safety that we should prepare in advance to deal with these calamities: it would be useless to wait until hostilities are threatened as it will take many months to train some of the volunteer helpers. We appeal, therefore, with confidence for volunteers, both men and women to enrol for training and service in this necessary task of self-preservation.[vii]

For most people, however, the prospect of war still seemed remote. The attendance at the first lecture on anti-gas precautions by the past president of Richmond Rotary in April 1937 'was so meagre that it was decided not to proceed with the lectures unless a larger number attended'. It probably did not help that women were not invited.

The Air Raid Precautions Committee, however, pressed ahead with its plans. Brigadier Arthur Shakespeare, late of the Royal Engineers, was appointed in early 1938 at the salary of £400 per annum to organise air-raid precautions (ARP) within the borough.[*]

By July 1938 the Air Raid Precautions Committee was looking for 538 ARP wardens alone. There was also a chronic shortage of drivers, even though affluent Richmond had a much higher proportion of car owners than the national average.[viii]

In addition a number of essential buildings had been sandbagged and made gas proof, including the Town Hall, the Petty Sessions Court, the

---

[*] It is almost impossible to give any idea of what a wartime pound is worth in modern terms. A very rough estimate might be to multiply every figure by fifty. Older readers will remember that the pound was then divided into twenty shillings (abbreviated as *s*) and subdivided again into twelve pennies (*d*).

Clinic and Public Baths. The public baths, in Parkshot, were a key part of the preparations. In addition to the gas decontamination areas, other parts of the building were to become the principal mortuary where the bodies of the victims were to be kept. Meanwhile the Poppy Factory was assembling 36,000 gas respirators for distribution if required.[ix]

Writing to volunteers, Brigadier Shakespeare summed up their duties in optimistic style:

> The main object of ARP is to keep the life and work of the nation in action to as great an extent as possible....experience in Spain and China has obviously shown that air bombardment on residential areas is not an effective or quick way of winning a war, provided reasonable precautions are taken.[x]

When Hitler threatened to annex the Sudetenland in September and October 1938, the Home Office urged local councils to expedite their air-raid preparations.

Councillors on Richmond's Civil Defence Committee, formerly the Emergency Committee, responsible for preparing the town for attack, and ensuring that the air-raid precautions ran smoothly during the war

On 30 September the Committee noted:

The construction of trench shelters for 4,300 persons has begun and these trenches have reached various stages of completion. Every available man was engaged for this purpose from the Employment Exchange, the Corporation's workmen and Contractors' employees. Mechanical diggers were also being used. The work was pressed forward with the utmost expedition by day and night.

Digging out the shelter on Richmond Green, September 1938

The Home Office supervised the Council's preparations. There are several files at The National Archives that show how closely Whitehall got involved. Central government was particularly insistent that local councils prepared for gas, with the correct number of ARP stations, and that the shelters had the right thickness of walls. In fact, in Richmond at least, there was considerable over-provision of shelters and other facilities. The greatest failure – and this was also true elsewhere – was to assume that people would not want to take shelter for hours at a time, so little or no provision was made for the comfort of shelterers.[xi]

Even at the end of March 1939 the Air Raid Precautions Committee noted that there was still a considerable shortage of volunteers and that there had been a very poor response at a recruitment meeting held at the Town Hall. Yet, a month later, recruitment increased. During April alone 134 men and 93 women volunteered.[xii] There was now an increasing realization that war was inevitable.

[i]   *Towards a Plan for Richmond* (1945), p2. For more about the Plan see Chapter 11.
[ii]   Mee, Arthur, *Surrey* (Hodder & Stoughton, 1938), p258. Plan, p12.
[iii]   Palmer, William, *Wanderings in Surrey* (Skeffington, 1949), p24.
[iv]   These figures are extrapolated from the 1931 Census and 1939 National Registration data, available on the Vision of Britain Through Time website www.visionofbritain.org.uk.
[v]   Quoted in Gardiner, Juliet, *The Blitz: the British under attack* (Harper, 2010), p1.
[vi]   Draft scheme of 29 October 1936.
[vii]   Draft scheme. Letter of 1 February 1938 to ratepayers from the Mayor.
[viii] *Richmond Herald*, 9 January 1937. ARP Sub-Committee, 9 July 1938.
[ix]   ARP Sub-Committee, 30 September 1938. TNA HO 207/798.
[x]   Letter from Brig A T Shakespeare, 24 February 1939.
[xi]   The references for the files at TNA are HO 207/798, 988, 1040.
[xii]   Letter from E M Neave, town clerk of Richmond, 10 April 1937 in Richmond Rotary Press Cuttings, 1935-1940; Air Raid Precautions Committee, 31 March 1939; Air Raid Precautions Committee, 28 April 1939.

CHAPTER 2 – *Taking Shelter*

War was declared on Sunday 3 September 1939. At 11am people crowded around their wireless sets to hear the Prime Minister, Neville Chamberlain, declare in particularly mournful tones that Britain was now at war with Germany. Almost immediately air-raid sirens began to sound all over the London area. Elizabeth Groves was with her father who was a consultant at Richmond Royal Hospital in Kew Foot Road: 'We didn't hear the broadcast but very shortly after eleven we heard the air-raid sirens. I suggested we went back home immediately to mother – we even ran some of the way. That first time we went to the shelter on Richmond Green. The shelter was crammed with people and their pets. There was little fear. People were just anxious.' And sixteen-year-old Jack Tuckwell made his way to a shelter in Old Deer Park where, he recalled, 'there was a general level of panic...everyone thought they would be obliterated upon the sound of the alarm.'[i]

Members of the First Aid Post at the Star and Garter Home on Richmond Hill, ready for action in November 1939

The authorities feared that the Germans would immediately launch devastating air raids, and would cause great loss of life. In fact for nine months, in what became known as the Phoney War nothing much happened.

On 10 May 1940 there were two developments that dramatically changed things. The first was the appointment of the First Lord of the Admiralty,

Winston Churchill, as Prime Minister after increasing concerns among MPs over how the War was being fought. Then, across the Channel the Wehrmacht launched a massive attack through the Low Countries into France, which within six weeks saw the fall of France and the evacuation of British forces from Dunkirk. Britain now stood alone against the Nazis.

On 14 May, the Home Secretary, Anthony Eden, broadcast an appeal for men to join a new body, the Local Defence Volunteers, which would become better known as the Home Guard. Eden had expected a poor response. But the opposite was true: in Richmond alone 800 men queued at the police station in Red Lion Street to enlist. Most were veterans of the First World War, or even of the Boer War, who were too old to join-up but not too old to fight. In the words of their commander, Lt Col A E Redfern, they were all 'very much out of date, a bit short in the wind, and very rusty [but this was compensated] by their eagerness to get going.'[ii]

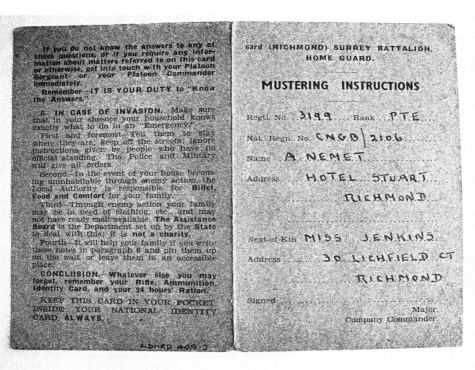

Tony Nemet's Home Guard muster card. Mr Nemet was a Hungarian refugee scientist who was not allowed to travel outside Richmond, which prevented him from going on many training exercises.

Many of the restrictions introduced in the weeks after the declaration of war had now been relaxed, and children who had been sent to safety in the countryside had mostly returned home, but one of the most important developments was complete – the National Register, which was taken at the end of September 1939, to allow ration cards to be issued and identify adults to be called up for war service.[*]

From July 1940 the skies of southern England saw the Battle of Britain, when the Luftwaffe attempted, but failed, to gain air superiority prior to German landings on British soil. Over the course of the Battle of Britain Richmond saw its fair share of these dogfights. Marie Lawrence witnessed one such combat:

> We saw Jerry being fired at from the river bank and then Glasheen [work colleague] and I raced to the water's edge and followed Jerry as they were firing. Then we saw three Spitfires after him and low. The first one fell out injured unfortunately. Then the other two raced after Jerry and went after him into a cloud.[iii]

The first bombing raids (the Blitz) on British towns followed in late August. Richmond was first attacked in the early hours of 9 September when High Explosive bombs fell on 35 Mount Ararat Road, and on 36 Marchmont Road on Richmond Hill. There were no casualties. Marie Lawrence wrote in her diary for that day:

> We heard several [bombs drop], we sat up in bed, we were so tired. Then suddenly a plane came right overhead, and, at the same moment there was a noise of the big gun in the Park and then a whistling sound as the bomb came down. I pulled the clothes over my head and yelled and then crashing and a roar, then silence. It was the most awful thing I have ever known.[iv]

A bomb had dropped on the nearby allotments destroying a chicken house. Fortunately nobody was hurt.

As a result of pre-war planning, Richmond's residents had a choice of places to shelter from air raids. There was a variety of public shelters open to anyone, designed to accommodate people who for one reason or another did not have a shelter of their own or were caught away from home while shopping or travelling to work. Schools provided shelters for pupils, which were also open in the evenings for local people. Where houses had gardens – and many in Richmond did – homeowners were

---

[*] The evacuation of Richmond children is discussed in Chapter 8.
The national register is available at www.findmypast.co.uk.

encouraged to build 'Anderson shelters' out of corrugated iron to accommodate the family. Some people preferred to convert basements instead.

Yet, surprisingly, most residents chose to do nothing. A survey conducted by the Council in December 1940 found that about thirty per cent had built Anderson shelters or the equivalent, that ten per cent used the public shelters, and that around sixty per cent had made no provision at all. They sheltered under the stairs or under the dining room table.[v]

Whichever shelter was chosen there was no guarantee of surviving a direct hit. However, shelters offered at least some protection against bombs and particularly the side effects like blast and splinters, and also gave a feeling of safety. For many people there must have been an air of fatalism that you could do little if the 'bomb had your name on it'. There are a number of stories in the local papers about residents who were away the night the shelter was destroyed or, more unfortunately, who had changed their routine with disastrous effect. Mrs Danby and her daughters, who were killed when a land mine dropped on Peldon Avenue in October 1940 were reported as having: 'been in the habit of going to a shelter and this was the first night they had failed to do so.'[vi]

At home

Certainly the most comfortable option – if perhaps the most dangerous – was to remain in your home, where it was likely to be warm and dry. As Betty and Gwen Watts's mother said: 'We'll take our chances. We stay together as a family; we either live or die together.' The twin sisters, who lived with their parents and siblings in Manor Grove, took shelter on mattresses under the dining room table or under a nearby dresser.

Aleksandra Parry-Jones, from Palmerston Road, remembered: '[We were] not as scared as much as I thought. There was a great craze in those days for doing jigsaws. So when there was bombing going on we'd sit doing our jigsaws, each on a big tray, and when we heard a lot of bombs coming down, we'd go into the hallway and carry on doing our jigsaws.'[vii]

By the beginning of 1941 householders were offered the chance to install Morrison shelters, which were basically wood and wire boxes in which to shelter during raids.[*] Despite their flimsy nature they proved very effective in withstanding the collapse of buildings. Unless you qualified for a free one, Morrison shelters cost £7 12s each. Take up was slow – in the first few months of 1941 only fourteen had been sold in Richmond and another 141 had been installed free of charge.[viii]

Many more householders – such as Marie Lawrence's parents – built a shelter in their garden. Named after Sir John Anderson, the government minister responsible for air-raid precautions, these were designed to accommodate up to six people. They were based on the use of curved and straight galvanised corrugated steel panels, which could be put together simply. A small drainage sump was often incorporated in the floor to collect rainwater seeping into the shelter – they were often very damp and cold. The shelters were buried four-foot deep in the soil and then covered with more soil over the roof. The earth banks were often planted with vegetables and flowers. The internal fitting out of the shelter was left to the owner. Marie Lawrence's father was a handyman and took considerable trouble to make the shelter in their garden as homely as possible. In her diary on 12 October 1940, she wrote: 'Dad has put a door on our shelter and we have the curtains on rings now and it is very good.' A few days later she noted that he had wallpapered the whole shelter. Jack Tuckwell remembers that the family Anderson shelter was quite safe, snug and with bunk-beds. He used to spend evenings there with his mother and sister.[ix]

Anderson shelters were issued free to all householders who earned less than £5 a week. Otherwise they cost £7. Richmond Council ordered 4,200 in May 1939 and others were erected during the war itself.[x]

An alternative was the basement. Basements were not recommended, because few had a second or emergency exit or much in the way of lighting. In order to help rescue parties, householders were expected to chalk the fact they were sheltering in a basement, and the numbers to be found there. But few did.

Offices, particularly those in converted houses, often had basements. Pamela Bousfield's father had an office on Richmond Green and turned 'the large basement into a roomy air raid shelter, with great wooden

---

[*] For those without the necessary skills, help in assembling the Morrison shelters could be obtained from the Boy Scouts. There is one on display at the Imperial War Museum, which looks like a very large rabbit hutch.

16

beams supporting the ceiling…we soon got into a routine of going down there when the siren sounded at about 6 p.m. with our books, food, radio, sewing and my school homework; then upstairs again for breakfast after the "all clear".'*xi

Marie Lawrence worked at Langholm Lodge on Petersham Road where there was a basement shelter. On 24 October 1940 she noted: 'We had two raids today. This afternoon we heard machine gunning and George [a work colleague] and I ran below for shelter. I never ran so much in all my life…'**

Away from home

Public and communal shelters, for people who had no other shelter or who were caught when a raid broke out, came into their own during the Blitz in the autumn and winter of 1940. Initially these shelters were pretty basic – often no more than deep trenches – but as the war progressed, and under pressure from their users, matters improved. They were really designed to provide shelter only during raids, but in Richmond, as elsewhere, people spent many nights there.

Each council was supposed to supply places for 15 per cent of its population. In this respect Richmond was particularly well supplied. In May 1941 E P M Harrison, the Ministry of Home Security's Assistant Regional Technical Adviser, noted: 'Richmond already possesses public and communal shelters far in excess of its quantum.' The largest shelter was on Richmond Green on the site of what was planned to be an underground car park. It was originally hoped to provide shelter for 2,000 people (with another 800 to be accommodated in the Old Deer Park), but by May 1939 this target had been reduced to a more manageable 642.xii

Because they were public shelters, certain standards of behaviour were to be expected. Richmond Council and the local papers spent a lot of time fussing over this. In September 1940, for example, the council minutes

---

* Pamela Bousfield's maiden name was Calvert Smith and the firm of solicitors is still in business on the Green.
**Several shelters still survive in local gardens. The author is aware of an exceptionally large one in Kew where the owner offers occasional tours for local schoolchildren.

recorded that 'notices have been exhibited in all public shelters prohibiting smoking and the practice of congregating in the entrances; with regard to the admission of dogs to public shelters the notices say that it is at the discretion of the shelter marshals.'[xiii]

Each shelter was under the control of a volunteer shelter marshal and his deputy, who were expected to maintain morale as well as order. There was always a shortage of such people. In November 1940 the *Richmond Herald* included an appeal from the Chief Shelter Marshal Harold Ball. Ball was headmaster of Holy Trinity School, and wanted to create 'a family party spirit' in every shelter. 'We need educated people possessing big hearts and capable of administering to the needs of the people, with an uppermost thought for the human side of the story. My chief aim is to make them happy; to maintain public morale.'[xiv]

There were other ways to maintain morale. The library staff discussed providing books to shelterers, but it is not clear whether they actually did so. In addition volunteers provided entertainment to the men and women in the shelters. The *Richmond and Twickenham Times* suggested that 'what was done was a proper antidote to the noise and other drawbacks of the night outside'. A story described how a Police Concert Party visited the shelters under the arches of Richmond Bridge and then at the Town Hall: 'They made quite a prepossessing appearance in their smart scarlet evening jackets with navy blue lapels, boiled shirts, white button holes and dandy sashes', providing a 'thoroughly entertaining show' with a mixture of comic turns and singing accompanied by violins. 'Gunfire was vigorous though unheeded during the concert and it was still prevalent as the party made its way to the Town Hall shelter to give a second turn.'[*][xv]

Meanwhile more fun was taking place at the shelter on Richmond Green where conditions 'were not as good as those in the other shelter, but that made the entertainment arranged all the more welcome'. Here 'A mixed programme that appealed to the various standards of taste in the audience had been arranged, but proceedings were informal and closed, so that sleepers could "bed down", at 9pm.' There was community singing together with records played on a radiogram.[xvi]

---

[*] The headline to this story in the *Richmond and Twickenham Times* was 'Cheerful Hours'. Dandy sashes appear to have been similar to cummerbunds. One wonders how the police had men to spare during the air raids.

Many of the public shelters were very unsatisfactory places in which to spend much time, because they were designed as temporary refuges, and because the Council (and presumably the government for whom they were acting as agents) did not want to encourage people to spend much time in them. They were damp, chilly and badly lit.

The worst problem was damp, which affected almost every shelter and was rather a disincentive to shelterers. Five-year-old Mary Buck remembered that from August 1940 she and her mother and siblings went to the shelters in Windham Road Recreation Ground every night until October when it started to get cold and damp: 'After that my brother and I slept under the kitchen table and my mother and sister slept under the stairs.' Betty Watts was diagnosed with 'diphtheria of the throat' after spending too many nights in public shelters. The Council's Emergency Committee minuted in December 1940 that they were 'fully alive to the urgency of the problem but are handicapped by the shortage of skilled labour and materials'.

An entrance to the shelter on Richmond Green. It could accommodate 600 people, but it was rarely full.

Things slowly improved. When one of the Regional Directors of Air Raid Precautions, Sir Edward Evans, visited the shelter on Richmond Green in December 1940 he described it as: 'one of the finest trench shelters he had seen.' He examined with interest a part of the shelters, which had suffered from dampness and had been successfully treated, and another that was waiting to be made waterproof.[xvii]

It was not until October and November 1940 that matters began to improve. One of the first acts was to provide basic sanitation in all the 65 public and communal shelters, as well as lighting in the larger ones. Cura paraffin stoves were installed in the shelters on Richmond Green and the Old Deer Park on the basis of one stove for every 25 people.[xviii]

The final step in making the shelters seem permanent was the introduction of bunks. In November 1940 the Council agreed to order 7,000 bunks at the cost of 14s each. By the end of the month five hundred bunks were arriving each week. They were to be three-tiered bunks, with the middle bunk so constructed that it could fold up to be used as a seat during the day. The disadvantage was that they took quite a lot of space. At the same time it was agreed to introduce shelter tickets, allowing individuals to reserve particular bunks. 'A holder of a season ticket must not absent himself for more than four consecutive days [and he had] the responsibility of keeping the beds and bedding clean.'[xix]

Inevitably there were grumbles from shelterers. An elderly resident complained that in one Richmond shelter a woman had established a couch on which she put her two boys aged about 10 and 12 years to sleep every night, while others took deck chairs there, 'leaving so little space that sometimes old people have to stand...It's quite right for little children to be put to bed there, but these older boys have pillow fights. I am quite content to sit on one of the seats provided. People should go to the shelter for safety, not for luxury.'[xx]

The public shelters were not very popular. As well as the dampness and other discomforts there was always the chance of mixing with one's social inferiors, an important consideration in class-conscious Richmond. The Vicar of St Mary Magdalene mused:

> I sometimes wonder whether all those in public shelters need to be there....those who can make reasonable arrangements in their own houses or shelters may well be serving their own and others' interest best by remaining there. At best a public shelter is a poor substitute for a healthy home as a safeguard against those illnesses that prey upon us in the winter months and the less crowded they are the safer and more comfortable will the shelters be for those

who must use them…The less time we spend in shelters and the
more we spend in sleep the better.[xxi]

Except on rare occasions the shelters were never filled to capacity. People
would rather remain in the open air than use them, unless they absolutely
had to. The *Thames Valley Times* noted in September 1940:

> Richmond Green trenches were not at all crowded for the lunch-
> hour warning, although many women who were out shopping were
> caught on their way home and waited with their laden baskets.
> Some, as no sound of guns or planes was heard, moved out in an
> obvious intention to reach home and keep as far as possible to their
> timetable.[xxii]

Reaction to raids

A constant problem was to get the public to take the raids seriously.
There were so many false alarms that people soon began to ignore the
sirens. Jack Tuckwell remembered that 'nobody took any notice of these
sirens' unless it was made immediately clear that the area was being
bombed. He added that people grew to accept that 'nothing would happen
until after dark'.[xxiii]

Another problem for the authorities was that people soon forgot to take
their gas masks with them or, worse, used the containers for purposes
other than they were intended. In February 1941 the papers warned
readers: 'Shelter marshals have the power to refuse admission to anyone
who does not carry a [gas] mask.'[xxiv]

And of course people were either caught away from a shelter or decided
to risk the bombs. Parents would dash to their children's school to collect
their offspring, or older children might be trusted to make their own way
home. The *Richmond Herald* told the story of a Mrs Copping who…

> …was at a cinema with one of her daughters when the raid began
> and after incendiaries had crashed through the roof of the cinema
> and the audience had been asked to leave, they started to walk
> home. They had not gone very far when she heard some bombs
> whistling down and they fell flat on the pavement. As the noise of
> the explosions died away they decided that they had better take
> shelter and went to a school playground where two shelters stood
> side by side. There was no room in the larger shelter, so they went
> into the smaller one.

It was the first time Mrs Copping had been in a shelter. Within half an hour a bomb fell just outside the entrance to the large shelter and another demolished four houses on the opposite side of the shelter. No one was trapped in the shelter. By midnight it became quieter and Mrs Copping and her daughter hurried on to their home, which was not far away. On the way to their house a German plane flew over and the guns fired on it. Mrs Copping said she finished her adventurous journey home at the double. A bomb had fallen in the road in which she lived, and a number of people had been killed.[xxv]

An air raid was in many ways like a terrible storm – 'the sky livid rent by jagged flashes, obscured by black clouds rolling across it or lit up by the reflected glow of fires, while the noise of bombs and guns echoed like the thunder of Mars, the god of war'.[xxvi]

For many like Marie Lawrence it was the noise that was the worst, the drone of the bombers, the throaty roar of the anti-aircraft guns, and rat-a-tat of the machine guns. On the night of the big raid on 29 November 1940 she wrote:

> There were fearful noises in the air and the guns banging. We did not know what to do and sat on. Hour after hour went by with terrible crashes. Before this some incendiaries dropped everywhere…We had a look out and saw two flares coming down on the allotments. Saw three fires in Richmond. All the place was lit up. Then we hear the planes come and circle and drop more bombs on the flames. There was crashing of glass and fumes everywhere. I said 'our greenhouses must have gone.' After the last lot I screamed. I could not help it.[xxvii]

During his first air raid Jack Tuckwell 'thought the world was going to end' because of the number of explosions, but was later told that the noise actually came from the anti-aircraft guns that were stationed nearby. For Aleksandra Parry-Jones, 'the most frightening part of it was not the explosion, but the whistle of the bombs coming down and when that got very bad we would go and sit in the hall away from the windows'.[xxviii]

For some, however, the air raids were more like a gigantic firework display, particularly when the Germans began to drop incendiaries designed to set buildings alight. Patricia Bousfield was watching with her father:

When the first of these hundreds of flaming torches landed on Richmond Green, my father and I were standing at the windows momentarily entranced by the amazing and spectacular sight, like a huge fireworks display, which was doing little harm on the open grass area of the Green. Then suddenly we realised that they were landing also in the back gardens of our old houses. We rushed to fetch our spades and dustbin lids and spent the next half-hour digging earth from the flowerbeds to extinguish several that had fallen in our garden.[xxix]

In many ways the shelters, in all their forms, were an insurance policy. Undoubtedly they saved some lives, prevented thousands of wounds, and kept morale up, although where the system was really tested – as happened in the East End – they were unable to prevent mass panic or serious injuries.

In general, however, the preparations made by Richmond and other councils ensured that the air raids of 1940 and 1941 were not as devastating as might have been expected. Although there remained considerable difficulties, the Council was surely right to congratulate itself when it minuted at the height of the Blitz:

The small number of casualties compared with the numbers of bombs dropped and the distribution of the material damage is a striking feature of these raids. The efficiency of all forms of public and private shelter which has been provided is proved beyond doubt.[xxx]

[i] Museum of Richmond, *Catalogue for Richmond at War: the Civilian Experience 1939-45* (Museum of Richmond, 1992), p3.
Jack Tuckwell interview with Alette Anderson, 22 June 2013.

[ii] Redfern, A E, *Reminiscences of the 63rd Surrey (Richmond) Battalion Home Guard* (Richmond,[1946]), p7.

[iii] Marie Lawrence diary, 9 October 1940.

[iv] Marie Lawrence diary, 9 September 1940.

[v] Emergency Committee, 14 December 1940. Of the 29,139 residents surveyed 17,730 were using no shelter; 7,308 were using private shelters in gardens and another 1,309 private sshelters in houses; 2,031 were using the public shelters and 1,013 used private communal shelters.

[vi] *Richmond Herald,* 8 December 1945.

[vii] Betty Watts interview with Alette Anderson, 5 May 2012.
Aleksandra Parry-Jones interview with Felix O'Kelley, undated.

[viii] Emergency Committee, 11 March 1941. Demand would greatly increase with the arrival of the V1 in the summer of 1944: see Chapter 6.

[ix] For more see www.andersonshelters.org.uk and the entry on Wikipedia.
Marie Lawrence's diary, 12 October 1940. Jack Tuckwell interview with Alette Anderson, 22 June 2013.

[x] *Richmond Herald,* 6 May 1939.

[xi] Patricia Bousfield contribution to BBC People's War Project.
www.bbc.co.uk/history/ww2peopleswar/stories/06/a4106206.shtml.

[xii] *Richmond Herald,* 6 May 1939.

[xiii] Emergency Committee, 10 September 1940.

[xiv] *Richmond Herald,* 23 November 1940.

[xv] *Richmond and Twickenham Times*, 23 November 1940.

[xvi] Ibid.

[xvii] Email from Mary Buck, 9 June 2014.
Betty Watts interview with Alette Anderson, 5 May 2012.
Emergency Committee, 14 December 1940.
Richmond and Twickenham Times, 14 December 1940.

[xviii] Emergency Committee, 10 September 1940, 14 December 1940, 11 February 1941

[xix] Emergency Committee, 9 November 1940.
Richmond and Twickenham Times, 30 November 1940.

[xx] *Richmond and Twickenham Times*, 14 September 1940.

[xxi] *Richmond Parish Magazine*, December 1940.

[xxii] *Thames Valley Times*, 24 September 1940.

[xxiii] Jack Tuckwell interview with Alette Anderson, 22 June 2013.

[xxiv] *Richmond and Twickenham Times*, 1 February 1941.

[xxv] *Richmond Herald*, 29 November 1940. She was possibly Mrs Coppen of 50 Halford Road.

[xxvi] Gardiner, Juliet, *The Blitz: the British under attack* (Harper, 2010), pxiv.

[xxvii] Marie Lawrence diary, 29 November 1940.

[xxviii] Jack Tuckwell interview with Alette Anderson, 22 June 2013.

[xxix] Patricia Bousfield contribution to BBC People's War Project.
www.bbc.co.uk/history/ww2peopleswar/stories/06/a4106206.shtml.

[xxx] Richmond Council minutes, 8 October 1940.

CHAPTER 3 - *The Ravaging of Richmond*

The series of air raids experienced by Richmond during 1940 and 1941 brought the War home in a way that nothing else would, although damage in the town was light compared with that in the East End, Coventry or Clydebank, let alone the German cities later subjected to carpet-bombing by the Allies.

Bomb damage to houses in Marchmont Road. The street was one of the first to be hit.

It has been suggested that the number of raids was due to the Luftwaffe using the town as a dumping ground for spare bomb loads or that the Star and Garter Home on the top of Richmond Hill was a bombing aiming point for the Luftwaffe. There seems to be no real evidence for either theory. The town's topography may have been more of a factor: the many parks and gardens could be easily identified from the air. Over half the bombs landed in the parks and other open spaces, which may explain why

Kew, Ham and Petersham, received proportionally more bombs than Richmond town itself. However, if you look at bomb maps for south-west London it is clear that Richmond was not a particular target. German aircraft tended to drop bombs along the roads and railways which criss-crossed the area, and the intensity of bombing grew ever less the further the area was from central London.[i]

On most occasions only a small number of bombs were dropped, but they could have devastating impact. One such raid took place on 1 October 1940 when St Paul's Congregational Church on Raleigh Road was destroyed by a single bomb. The blast also badly damaged houses nearby. In an extended retrospective article published in 1945, the *Richmond Herald* recalled that: 'shortly before [3am] it was reduced to a pile of rubble by a direct hit. This was the only bomb dropped in the area. It was thought that the plane from which it came had been hit by anti-aircraft shells...today little more than the foundations mark the site.'[ii]

Marie Lawrence, who lived in Castlegate a few minutes walk away, noted in her diary:
> [We] woke up to an awful whistling noise as if something was rushing through the air, then a dreadful bang which lifted us from our bunks [in the shelter in their garden]. We shouted we are hit the house will be gone. Anyway after noting our house had not been hit, we managed to sleep a little...There was a huge crater as big as the Manor Road allotments... All the houses facing look wrecks and their roofs look upset and the windows are gone. We saw Mr and Mrs James whose house is all holes and windows out. She looks terribly white and so does Mr James. I am terribly sorry for them. In fact the damage made me sick.[iii]

Mary Buck says: 'We were in the shelters the night St Paul's Church was bombed and I think I can still remember the noise it made and coming home in the morning to a house without windows.'[iv]

Courtlands and Peldon Avenue

The worst damage was caused by the two-thousand-kilogram mines that landed on the complex of flats at Courtlands and on houses in Peldon Avenue, off the Sheen Road, at 2.40am on 20 September 1940. The

Richmond Herald reporter thought: 'The area resembled part of Ypres in the last war.'[*]

Writing in 1945, the *Herald* remembered:
> Seen in early morning light Peldon Avenue presented a grotesque and terrible picture. In the centre of the roadway about halfway up the avenue was a huge gaping cavity caused by the mine. Rubble was piled up over the road and a few bricks by the cavity were the remains of three houses. The rest had completely disappeared. Not a house had escaped. They stood grotesquely with split walls, roofs blown clean away – most of them simply shells, filled with the wreckage of collapsed floors, ceilings and inner walls. Here and there a bed sprawled rakishly over a mound of debris. Clothing and contents of drawers were strewn widespread among them – the most moving of all – children's toys.[v]

Here was real tragedy. Among the casualties were a policeman's family: Lillian Maude Danby (aged 44) and her three daughters Margaret Ellen (aged 14), Stella Annie (13) and Sybil Lillian (11) of 15 Peldon Avenue:
> A policeman who was first on the scene collapsed on hearing that his three daughters had been killed. His wife crawled out from under the wreckage of her home to tell the workers that the children were underneath. They were found huddled together. A young son who had taken refuge under the stairs was found unhurt.[vi]

Mrs Danby later died of her wounds at Richmond Royal Hospital. Her daughters were all pupils at the Richmond County School for Girls, where the school history described them as being 'the best of pupils, pleasant, thoughtful, intelligent and had faced with cheerfulness and courage the difficulties of the war'.[vii]

Next door lived the Blackburn family. Their youngest daughter Audrey has vivid memories of that evening:
> My mother, my older sister, and my twin brother and I were asleep in our Anderson shelter in the garden. The explosion awakened me, and then the screams and cries of the trapped injured and dying mingled with the sounds of falling bricks and buildings and the

---

[*] A third land mine, which failed to explode, landed in Sandycombe Road, Kew. See Blomfield, David, and May, Christopher, *Kew at War* (Richmond Local History Society, 2009), p9.

shattering of glass. The silence which had followed the "All Clear" five or ten minutes earlier turned into a horrifying medley of terror and confusion. My mother managed to claw her way through the earth and debris which effectively blocked our only exit to the shelter, and called out that next-door's house was down - OUR house was down - they're ALL down!

... the family next door on our left were sleeping in the house that night: the mother, three daughters and a son. These children were much the same age as us and we played together. Sybil, Stella, Margaret and John Danby. All the girls were scholarship pupils at Richmond County School for Girls. The bodies of the mother and the girls were eventually recovered, but John was found safe and unharmed and he was brought to our shelter by the wardens, along with an elderly woman (I believe she was a Belgian refugee) and another woman.[viii]

Clearing up Peldon Avenue after the raid of 20 September 1940. It reminded one reporter of the devastation of Ypres in the First World War.

Daphne Harris was the ambulance driver who took the Belgian refugee, whose identity still remains a mystery, to Richmond Royal Hospital for treatment:

We heard afterwards that she, with her husband and son had come across the channel in a small boat and had just that day been moved into a house locally. It had been wrecked that night and she was our only patient. We assumed her family had been killed. I did what I could for her in the short journey to the Hospital. I have often wondered since what happened to her. It all seemed so tragic.[ix] *

After the war Courtlands was rebuilt and a new block of flats – Peldon Court – were constructed on the bombsite of Peldon Avenue.

Richmond blitzed

The worst raid occurred on between 7.30pm and 11.15pm on 29 November, with the greatest damage occurring before 8pm. That night the Luftwaffe was targeting towns across a wide swathe of West Middlesex and Northern Surrey.

Of Richmond the *Richmond Herald* wrote:
> On that night the Germans made a vain effort to wipe out the town by a concentrated attack of high explosive and firebombs. It was Richmond's most severe ordeal and for several hours bombs rained down in the centre of the town. Fires ranged everywhere, houses were pulverised into rubble; the air was heavy with the smell of burning…bombs rained down without regard to any particular target. Calls for the fire brigade were so many that it was difficult to keep trace of them. Every available piece of equipment was brought into use. Three fire floats were engaged in pumping water from the river and there were hosepipes everywhere. They wound through the streets and Richmond Hill like great snakes. It was like a scene from Dante's Inferno…[x]

Many buildings were either badly damaged or destroyed altogether. Chief among them was the Town Hall on Hill Street, which suffered a direct hit. The *Richmond and Twickenham Times* described the scene:
> The council chamber had been wrecked. Chairs and benches matched the fire-blackened debris from the roof and the charred

---

* The Belgian lady does not appear in the list of war deaths; so she must have survived.

panelling of the walls presented an ugly picture. Offices near the flames had escaped the damage, but water was pouring on to the desks and cupboards. Outside was a member of staff with a brown paper parcel under his arm. It contained all that was left of his office – books he had taken home the previous night to complete some work.[xi]

The Council Chamber at Richmond Town Hall, photographed shortly after the raid of 29 November 1940

Again there were major casualties. Because of heavy censorship at that time, the *Richmond and Twickenham Times* could allude only to the loss of life, not to the address:

> Four adults [actually five] and three children were killed when a public shelter received a direct hit. Among the injured was a girl, trapped by the legs, who talked cheerfully while rescue men worked for several hours to free her... She fainted after she was released, but her injuries were stated to be slight... A resident commented on the efficiency of the rescue parties, which were soon on the scene.

This bomb in fact fell on the British Legion Poppy Factory shelter killing Mrs Pamela Reddings, and her children Gwendolene (aged 15), Jean (11) and John (7). Other casualties were Ethel Lomas and her daughter Ivy as well as Edith Stuckey and Alice Morey.

The next day Marie Lawrence went into central Richmond:

> I walked up Paradise Road and when I came to a spare piece of ground opposite the schools where the school shelter was there was a huge crater and first two or three houses in Eton Street were down. The mess was dreadful, I walked on and came opposite the Town Hall when a sight greeted me. The road was full of pumps. The Town Hall was gutted although it looked all right from the front. Goslings next door is to the ground. The AFS [Auxiliary Fire Service] were fighting the fire in Kew Road when they were bombed and the high explosives fell on Bartons Store. He evidently thought it was Richmond Station. Wrights were bombed out at the back and many other shops...[xii] *

Members of the Home Guard helped rescue some of the stock from Bartons. According to Mr J H Halls, 'These included some of the display dummies...the next day it caused rather a laugh as a rumour went around that [we] had brought dead bodies out.'[xiii]

> The greatest urban myth of the War was that the German propagandist William Joyce, nicknamed Lord Haw Haw, would comment about individual raids, in each case showing particular local knowledge. Reporting on the raid of the 29 November, Joyce is supposed to have apologised for the destruction of Richmond, saying that the target was actually Battersea, but the Luftwaffe had mistaken the bend in the river. He also apologised for the destruction of the Royal Naval School on Richmond Green: 'We are sorry to have had to bomb the Naval School – so upsetting for the fathers at sea.'**[xiv]

---

* Goslings was a furniture shop, Bartons a drapers and Wrights a department store.

** Lord Haw Haw seems to have been fed 'duff gen' as the contemporary term was. In fact, the School had left Richmond as long ago as 1870.

16 April 1941

The last major bombing raid occurred on 16 April 1941. The *Richmond Herald* later summarised the evening's activities:

> Two bombs fell in Crown Terrace. Among the victims was a woman who was taking coffee to her husband on fire-watching duty and a woman in a passing motor car who was hit with a fragment of cement…the second bomb fell at the junction of Sheen Vale and the 'Bricklayer's Arms' and a man and a women in a passing motor car were among those injured, the woman fatally. The car was lifted from the road to the pavement by the force of the explosion.[xv]

> Mr and Mrs Thomas Sargeant and their little 10-year old daughter June who were in their Anderson Shelter [at 34 Crown Terrace] were killed by a direct hit. Mrs Hyde and her baby usually shared the shelter but were away. Mr Sargeant was on duty as a firewatcher and had gone in to see how his wife was getting on. Their house and the adjoining one were almost completely demolished, the roof and upper floor sloping down sharply, but a piano and other furniture on the ground floor could still be seen undamaged. Out of one of these two houses Mrs Ayling and her three children, two girls and a boy, emerged only slightly injured. Mrs Ayling had her leg and her head cut. They had been sheltering under the stairs. Mr Ayling was also away fire watching. Their Anderson shelter, with its bunks, was flattened by the direct hit…[xvi]

A few weeks later under the headline 'Military Target Bombed' the *Richmond Herald* included a photograph of the house in Crown Terrace with this caption:

> During a recent heavy night air blitz on the London area a heavy bomb crashed at the rear of one of the houses in Crown Terrace and… reduced to rubble and matchwood the modest homes of many working class people. A firewatcher and his wife and daughter were killed when the bomb wrecked their Anderson shelter.[xvii]

And then there was silence. For three years there were almost no raids on Richmond. The Luftwaffe was directed to operate on the Eastern Front and there were only sporadic raids on English towns. On 8 November 1943 bombs fell on Petersham, and on 19 February 1944 there was an attack on Richmond Lock. Neither raid was particularly serious.

[i]   Calculated from data in the Buildings Damage List prepared by the Borough Council after the war.

[ii]   *Richmond Herald*, 8 December 1945.

[iii]   Marie Lawrence diary, 1 October 1940.

[iv]   Mary Buck email to author, 9 June 2014.

[v]   *Richmond Herald*, 8 December 1945.

[vi]   Ibid. Her husband was PC John Charles Danby.

[vii]   Scudamore, Margaret, *The Richmond and East Sheen County School for Girls: a record 1861-1947* (Richmond, 1947), p33.

[viii]   Audrey Blackburn contribution to People's War Project www.bbc.co.uk/history/ww2peopleswar/stories/56/a6314456.shtml.

[ix]   Daphne Harris contribution to BBC People's War Project www.bbc.co.uk/history/ww2peopleswar/stories/44/a5148344.shtml.

[x]   *Richmond Herald*, 15 December 1945.

[xi]   *Richmond and Twickenham Times*, 7 December 1940. See also the Local History Note at www.richmond.gov.uk/local_history_old_town_hall.pdf.

[xii]   Marie Lawrence diary, 30 November 1940.

[xiii]   Museum of Richmond, *Catalogue for Richmond at War: the Civilian Experience 1939-45* (Museum of Richmond, 1992), p18.

[xiv]   *Richmond Herald*, 22 December 1940. Museum of Richmond, *Catalogue*, p24: Comment by Elizabeth Grove.

[xv]   *Richmond Herald*, 29 December 1945. The woman fatality was probably Jean Bingham of Barnes.

[xvi]   *Richmond and Twickenham Times*, 19 April 1941. The paper gave the wrong name for the daughter. She was actually Mabel Beatrice.

[xvii]   *Richmond Herald*, 10 May 1941.

CHAPTER 4 – *Dealing with the Consequences*

Richmond's air-raid precautions depended on teams, both men and women, who gave up their leisure hours to guard against fires, to chivvy residents to shelters, or to dig them and their possessions out if the worst happened. These were the men and women of the Air Raid Precautions (renamed from 1941 as the Civil Defence Service). Their teams were a mixture of people who had been assigned to civil defence work, but most were volunteers, like Margaret Scudamore, who had a difficult daytime job as headmistress of the County School for Girls in Parkshot, but in the evenings acted as a fire guard, looking out for falling incendiaries in the streets around her home in Marchmont Road.

For most it was a tedious chore, but others clearly relished the social side, the responsibility and perhaps the power, that inevitably came with the work. Judging from the large photograph album kept by Miss Margaret Aldred relating to the activities of V Warden Post, she thoroughly enjoyed her time in the ARP. She attended training courses, taught her own classes and probably organised her Post within an inch of its life. There were parties, a wedding when two assistant wardens married each other (and tragedy when the husband died suddenly a few months later), and clearly a great deal of companionship, coupled with a feeling she was doing valuable war work.[*]

In September 1940, there were 461 members of the ARP in Richmond, responsible for sounding the alerts and all clear, enforcing the blackout and making sure that civilians were in shelters during raids, and providing emergency aid to the wounded and destitute. According to Margaret Scudamore, they could also 'fit gas masks and make you believe that you could pass hours in reasonable comfort wearing them.'[i]

Each of the ten wards in the Borough had an ARP Warden's Post or office, which acted as a reception centre for the unfortunate people whose houses had been destroyed or damaged by bombing ('bombed out' in the phrase of the time), as well as a notice board where official news would be placed. In turn, each post was divided into sectors, with three to six wardens in each sector. Wardens were almost always local – it was essential that they knew their sector and the people living there.

---

[*] The album is now kept at the Local Studies Library.

WATCH ON RIVER & VALLEY
on Poppy Factory
roof. manned day
and night on alerts.
$\approx$ 50 feet up.

OCTOBER
1940

Sharpe in pillbox.

Aldred gazing into space.

Aldred.

Sharpshooting.

Mr. Morrison's watch.

Sharpe.

Molly Woolley - Telephonist

Front: Barstow, Mr. Morrison, Back: Hall Flack
Dawes and Chaff

Mr. Hughes.

Miss Patterson (telephonist) Miss Holmes

V Warden's Post, October 1940

35

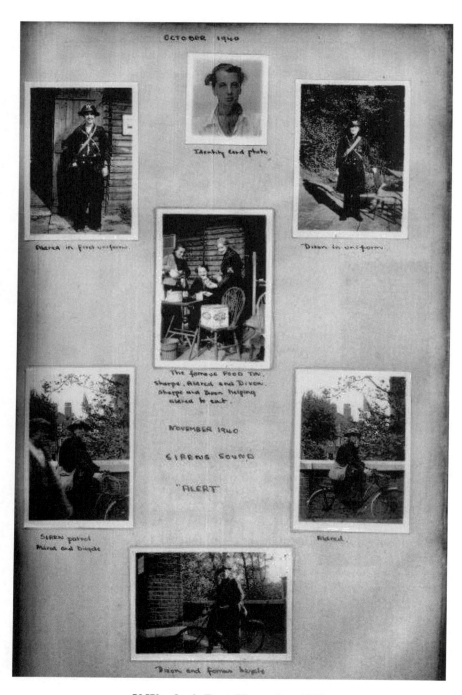

V Warden's Post, November 1940

Whenever the air-raid sirens sounded, the wardens would help people into the nearest shelter and then tour their sector, usually in pairs, at considerable risk from bombs, shrapnel and falling masonry. They would also check regularly on those in the air-raid shelters. In the aftermath of a raid, wardens would often be first on the scene, carrying out first-aid if there were minor casualties, putting out any small fires and helping to organise the emergency response.

A few wardens were full-time, but most were volunteers who carried out their ARP duties three nights a week as well as their full-time jobs. Laura Dance worked at the Warden's Post in King's Road:

> I did 24 hours on and 24 hours off. I had most of my meals at the depot. Everyone learnt to drive and was taught first aid and we played bridge and table tennis to keep ourselves occupied while we waited for alerts. We organised dances – we were known as the King's Road Glamour Girls.[ii]

At the beginning of the war, ARP wardens had no uniform, but wore their own clothes, with the addition of a steel helmet, Wellington boots and an armband. In May 1941 full-time and regular part-time wardens were issued with blue serge uniforms.[iii]

The rescue teams undoubtedly saved many lives as they scrambled to remove debris. Peter Winnall's father, Ted, was one such volunteer in Ham. One night a bomb landed on Craig Road:

> As Ted told it, he was met not just with the scene as described, but the remains of the house had rescue workers standing on them doing nothing. When asked, these 'rescue' men said that nobody who was in any of the houses could possibly still be alive. So Ted made some enquiries to find that three people were unaccounted for and that they used that other natural shelter in most houses, 'the Cupboard under the stairs'. Then he got someone to point out approximately where the stairs would be. With that information he commenced a solo dig. He continued this like an upside down mole until he could get a reply to his calls. That's where he spent the rest of that night digging away with his hands until he had located Grandma, her daughter and a grandchild. Then he directed the rest of the operation until they were brought out unhurt.[iv]

For his efforts Mr Winnall received a letter of thanks from Richmond's Mayor. No member of a rescue team locally received an official honour or award, although a resident from Ham, Herbert Alfred Mauncey, who was a volunteer driver with the Auxiliary Fire Service, was recommended for an award for saving the lives of local residents while fighting a fire in the Victoria Docks in March 1941.[v]

Personnel of a warden's post

Where possible, badly-damaged buildings were made safe for habitation again. Rarely were they demolished: just under 300 houses had to be bulldozed, less than two per cent of the town's housing stock. Much of this work was undertaken by Council workmen or building contractors employed by the Council. The work was praised after one raid:

> If there is one branch of the Council's work service which has received commendation, it is the department dealing with the repair of houses damaged by bombing. There is a shortage of labour, but the builders co-operate with the Council and their men were on the spot early in the morning doing essential first-aid work repairing the roofs. Windows were being repaired with a new kind of sheeting, something more substantial than felting hitherto used and white on both sides, making a better finish to the job.[vi]

Helping the dispossessed

The air raids impacted on people's lives in various ways. Some had been expected, while others could not have been anticipated.

The most immediate impact was on the victims of the raids and the houses they lived in. A network of reception centres was established across the borough to look after families who had been bombed out of their houses. These provided tea and comfort, helped people find accommodation and replaced papers and ration books that had been lost in the devastation. A reporter from the *Richmond and Twickenham Times* visited one, where he found 'many men, women and children homeless, but they were not disheartened. A rest centre had been opened and members of the WVS were on the spot with offers of help and advice. Rescue workers were moving furniture into the street in readiness for despatch to local storage till its owners find a new home...'[*vii]

Audrey Blackburn's family house in Peldon Avenue was wrecked:
> With no papers, money, clothes – nothing at all except the nightclothes we were wearing – we were taken to a primary school in Darell Road, Kew, where an assortment of mostly quite inappropriate garments were distributed to us, and then transported to Matthiae's Restaurant on Kew Road for a full English breakfast with a silver service and the waitresses in full uniform. This must have been about 9am – a truly marvellous gesture by the restaurateur and his staff.[viii]

However, Social Services were often far less sympathetic to the plight of those who had been bombed out. Audrey remembered that 'my parents and the father of the young family killed next door were treated like criminal paupers; they were asking for help when, it was implied, they didn't deserve it – they must look after themselves.'[ix]

The Richmond Royal Hospital, in Kew Foot Road, was required to keep fifty beds free for people injured in the raids. ** Only once, however – on the night of the big raid on 29 November – were the beds really needed.

---

* A depository to house furniture and effects from those made homeless by the bombing was set up in a shop next to the Town Hall, which sadly was totally destroyed during the raid of 29 November 1940.
** Whitehall paid for the beds, and when the grant was withdrawn in 1945 the hospital became bankrupt.

Thirty-one patients were admitted that night and another sixty men and women were treated in out-patients.[x]

Across the Chertsey Road in Parkshot there was a feeding centre at the County School for Girls, which would be used to provide meals if large numbers of people had been bombed out: 'Pots, pans and tea urns, dishes, cups, cutlery and even babies' feeding bottles were stored in large quantities in the little room off the gymnasium.' There were also two field kitchens, and three teams of pupils practised using them if there was no gas or electricity.[xi]

Flight from the East End

An unforeseen emergency was the sudden arrival in September 1940 of nearly a thousand poor Londoners fleeing the destruction caused by the Blitz. It was part of a mass movement away from the East End. Many thousands fled into Epping Forest, while others made it as far as Reading and Oxford. Frank Lewey, the Mayor of Stepney, who arranged the despatch of thousands of desperate men, women and children, wrote later that he and his staff were... 'far too busy to keep records of the evacuees. It was all we could do to get them out of London fast enough. We did not know where they had all gone, or all who had gone there, except that one hundred and fifty had gone to Ealing, two hundred and thirty to Richmond and so on. Then of course we began to be besieged by relatives who had no idea where their loved ones had vanished to; and we could not tell them.'[xii]

In Richmond they arrived at short notice on 12 September. According to the *Richmond and Twickenham Times*, '1,000 men, women and children... arrive[d], after a four hour journey down river by barge or in pleasure launches. The first relay arrived at about 12 o'clock; a later party were landing just as an air raid warning sounded and so had to take shelter under the arches by the riverside immediately, and the last 600 arrived so late that they could not be billeted on Thursday, but had to spend the night at the cinema sleeping on the chairs or the floor.[xiii]

Finding accommodation for the refugees was not easy. Homeowners were reluctant to take in strangers, particularly those from a different social class. Mayor H A Leon appealed for help:

> Within the last few days many families whose homes in another part of London have been damaged in the recent air raids have

come to Richmond. They have been placed in Richmond households where I know they will receive a warm welcome and the utmost practical help in their distress. Inconvenience will inevitably be felt by the householders on whom they were billeted, but this inconvenience is negligible compared with the unhappy circumstances of those who have had to leave their homes. I appeal to all to their utmost to meet this emergency in a happy spirit of co-operation.[xiv]

Responding to the appeal, Margaret Scudamore played host to a little girl: 'who looked with disfavour on the bathing facilities provided and such innocuous foodstuffs as we could muster, and longed only for the joys of her companionable cul-de-sac and piquant pickles.'[xv]

Not everybody was so hospitable. Writing after the war, the *Richmond Herald* remembered:

Some householders accepted evacuees reluctantly and did nothing to make these people comfortable, with the result that a large number of East Enders left their billets at night and slept in public shelters and walked the streets by day. Families became separated and the big problem was to find accommodation for large families. Often families had to be billeted in different houses and the fact that they wanted to meet each other during the day led to further trouble. Gradually these were smoothed out… considering the large numbers of persons dealt with there were few cases of dirty conditions.[xvi]

Most East Enders soon returned home because they were homesick or just worried about what had happened to their homes and possessions. Those that remained were absorbed into the local population and many made their lives in Richmond.[xvii]

To an extent the events described in this chapter had been anticipated. Indeed, there was an over-provision of civil defence locally, although nobody at the time thought that this was the case and sensibly prepared for the worst. Only the raid of 29 November 1940 really tested the system, and even here, by and large, the organisation worked well.

[i] Richmond Council minutes, 10 September 1940. Also included in the number were 48 council workmen 'doing their normal work'.
Scudamore, Margaret, *The Richmond and East Sheen County School for Girls: a record 1861-1947* (Richmond, 1947), p37.

[ii] Museum of Richmond, *Catalogue for Richmond at War: the Civilian Experience 1939-45* (Museum of Richmond, 1992), p6.

[iii] The paragraph is based on the BBC People's War webpage at www.bbc.co.uk/history/ww2peopleswar/timeline/factfiles/nonflash/a6651425.shtml See also Scudamore, p37.

[iv] Peter Winnall contribution to the BBC People's War Project www.bbc.co.uk/history/ww2peopleswar/stories/16/a4059416.shtml.

[v] TNA HO 250/26. In the end it was decided that he should not receive an award.

[vi] *Thames Valley Times*, 12 March 1941.

[vii] *Richmond and Twickenham Times*, 12 March 1941.

[viii] Audrey Blackburn contribution to the BBC People's War Project www.bbc.co.uk/history/ww2peopleswar/stories/56/a6314456.shtml.

[ix] Ibid.

[x] Richmond Royal Hospital Annual Report (1940), p4.

[xi] Scudamore, p31.

[xii] Quoted in Gardiner, Juliet, *The Blitz: the British under attack* (Harper, 2010), p127. See also TNA file HO 186/342.

[xiii] *Richmond and Twickenham Times*, 14 September 1940.

[xiv] Ibid.

[xv] Scudamore, p47.

[xvi] *Richmond Herald*, 29 December 1945.

[xvii] See also Blomfield, David, and May, Christopher, *Kew at War* (RLHS, 2009), pp25 -26, and Chave, Leonard, and Lee, J M, *Ham & Petersham in Wartime* (RLHS, 2011), pp38-39.

CHAPTER 5 – *Everyday Life in WW2*

The lives of everybody in Britain were affected by the war. The government – national and local – controlled lives to a far greater degree than would have been thought acceptable in peacetime. The British people were told what they could eat and wear, where they should work, how to spend their leisure hours, and even what to think. And although there was considerable grumbling this direction was overwhelmingly accepted. It was accepted as being necessary and, because everybody from dukes to dustmen was affected equally, it was perceived as largely being fair. That is not to say there was not a black market, nor that there was no petty crime – bombed houses for example had to be protected against looters.

Food rationing was introduced in 1939 and lasted, surprisingly, until 1954 when meat and bacon finally came off ration, although it was at its most severe in the later years of the war and in the early post-war period. Everybody was issued with a ration book.

Even when food was not rationed, it could be in very short supply. Eggs, for example, were very hard to come by, unless you knew someone who kept chickens, Dorothy Murphy-Grumbar remembered:

> Powdered eggs were sent from America in tins. There were tiny bits of shell in the powdered egg. The joke was that it was what happened to old ping-pong balls. In an American film 'Moon over Miami', when a character stubbed out a cigarette in a fried egg, there was a shocked gasp from the audience.[i]

A wartime wedding cake made out of cardboard by Matthiae's Restaurant.

Every square inch of land was dug up to grow food. School playing fields and the Little Green in Richmond were among the open spaces turned into allotments. Domestic gardens too were converted to food. Elsie Erlebach's father kept rabbits and chickens, while John Leach's parents grew 'beans in the small patch of earth in the yard' behind the family's shop on Lower Mortlake Road.[ii]

There were of course ways to get round food shortages – wittingly and unwittingly. An unofficial black market grew up where allotment holders sold their produce to hungry locals, and later in the War, when American troops were in Britain preparing for D-Day, the GIs would occasionally offer friends overstocks from their wonderfully well-provided kitchens. Unfortunately, this could lead to problems with the authorities, as Mrs Pacitto, whose family ran Mylo's Ice Cream Parlour, remembered well:

> The Italian-American GIs used to come in and give us a bit of bacon or nice meat that they had. I would take it home to cook and neighbours would follow the smell into the house. One day one of the neighbours told the food provisions office and they got onto Daddy and he was in trouble.'[iii]

Although there was considerable grumbling about rationing and the food was dull and boring, nobody starved and most people were better nourished as a result.

Restaurants were less affected by rationing, but they were restricted in what they could serve, and from 1942 the most they could charge for a meal was five shillings. Richmond had a number of small restaurants, most notably Valchera's Italian Restaurant on the Quadrant (where McDonalds is today), and hotel dining rooms, as well as pubs, tearooms, such as the Lyon's Corner House on George Street, and fish and chip shops. Before the War eating out had been the preserve of the middle classes, but now, because of rationing and the travails of everyday life in wartime, eating-out boomed as workers sought a quick and filling meal.

At the same time the Government encouraged local councils to set up Orwellian sounding Communal Feeding Centres, which are better known as British Restaurants, to provide subsidised meals for local workers. By 1943 there were four such restaurants in Richmond. The largest was at Carrington Lodge on Sheen Road, which opened in March 1943. It could seat 120 in a room painted grey, but with art 'worth thousands' on the walls. A main course cost nine pence; a sweet was tuppence, bread a penny, soup also tuppence, and a cup of tea a penny ha'penny. Although bread was not rationed it was often in short supply, so to encourage people to eat potatoes instead they were provided free with the soup. The cooking was undertaken by members of the Women's Voluntary Service (WVS) under the supervision of dinner ladies from Gainsborough Road School in Kew. It was cheap and cheerful and provided a nutritious if not, by today's standards, a particularly tasty meal.[iv]

Scrap

Even if an item was not rationed it was generally in very short supply. It was drummed into people not to waste anything and to reuse or recycle where possible. Today the older generation is still instinctively reluctant to throw anything away just in case it can be used again. This largely comes from their wartime experiences.

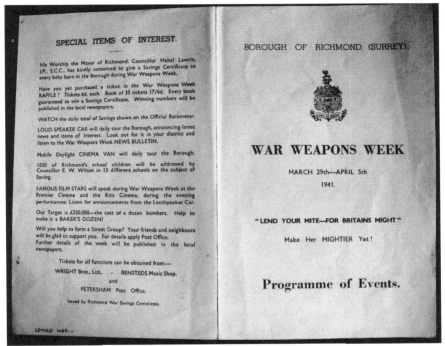

Programme for War Weapons Week, 1941

There were several campaigns to encourage people to donate metal and other items. In Richmond much of the collecting was done by members of the Women's Voluntary Service at Eton Lodge on Paradise Road.[v] It was said that the metal was to be used in making aircraft and other weapons, but in fact it was not suitable for the purpose. The first campaign, in the summer of 1940, was for aluminium pans. Lord Beaverbrook, Minister for Aircraft Production, appealed to the women of Britain: 'The need is instant. The call is urgent. Our expectations are high.' Every household, from Buckingham Palace to the smallest cottage, made its contribution, and in some cities the traffic was held up by mountains of aluminium. One old lady, parting with her only hot water bottle, was clear that she wanted it made into a Spitfire, not a Hurricane, because, after careful study of the papers, she had decided that they were the best planes.

Richmond's archives were not exempt. In 1941 and 1942 collections for scrap paper saw the borough's librarian, William Piper, send 90 percent of the town's nineteenth-century rate books for pulping. Equally serious was the removal for scrap of the Russian cannon from the Crimean War that stood on Richmond Green.

In September 1941 the Ministry of Supply wrote to Richmond Council requiring all unnecessary iron or steel railings to be removed for scrap for use in iron and steel foundries and asking for the full co-operation of all local authorities. The council began the process of identifying and removing railings. Most appeals against the removal of the railings were dismissed, although in March the following year there was heated debate in the council chamber about removing the railings from Richmond Green. The railings here had been in position for over a century and added considerably to its charm. In the end those opposite the eighteenth-century Maids of Honour Row were kept and the others were removed.[vi]

Savings weeks

Considerable efforts were made to link local people with the wider effort. Local war heroes were treated like royalty. In Richmond there was the air ace Wing Commander Brendan 'Paddy' Finucane. Finucane's links with the town were tenuous, Almost as soon as his family arrived from Dublin Paddy joined the RAF, although his fiancé, Jean Woodford, lived two doors down from his family's home in Castlegate. Before he was killed over the English Channel on 15 July 1942 he had shot down 28 enemy aircraft and had become the youngest ever Wing Commander in the RAF. He was just 21. A block of flats, Finucane Court on the Lower Mortlake Road, is named in his honour. Paddy's youngest brother Kevin went to Sheen County School. His friend John Leach remembered: 'Kevin was a hero with the girls and I often had to wait for him after school as the girls queued up to kiss him… I held his bike and watched.'*[vii]

* Less attention was paid to Captain John Randle VC, who lived on Queen's Road. Randle was awarded his medal posthumously for action at the battle of Kohima on 4 May 1944. There is a memorial in St Peter's Church, Petersham.

Lᵗ B.E. FINUCANE D.F.C.   (R.AAF) SQUADRON

**A charcoal drawing by Claude Orde of Paddy Finucane,
Richmond's great war hero**

Another way of involving the public were Savings Weeks in which towns and cities raised money to 'buy' aircraft and ships for the RAF and Royal Navy, or bought savings bonds. The first of these campaigns took place in the summer of 1940 when £5,000 was raised to buy a Spitfire. As the campaign developed almost every society, club and pub in the borough were involved. Boatmen on the river offered a day's takings to the Fund amounting to £59. There were dances, garden parties and street performances by children. Small bracelets made from the bullet-proof

47

windscreens of crashed Spitfires were sold for two shillings each. Nasty Crash clubs were set up with members promising to subscribe a penny or two for every enemy aircraft brought down during September.

There was a big collection box at Lion House in Red Lion Street bearing a model of a fighter plane. Two shops selling bric-a-brac in aid of the Fund were opened in George Street and on Hill Street, opposite the Town Hall, which 'no one could miss seeing it bears the name of the Fund in the national colours, has fighter planes painted on a side wall and contains air raid relics in the window.'

Undoubtedly the highlight of the campaign was the arrival of two Dornier bombers, which were displayed on Little Green. The first was in 400 pieces, so it must have left something to the imagination. It was joined a few days later by a Dornier 17, which had crashed-landed after bombing Buckingham Palace. Visitors paid a penny or two to inspect the planes.

By the end of September constant raids and air-raid warnings began to affect fundraising. The papers reported that 'prevailing circumstances have somewhat hampered the efforts of the organisers'. Yet the raids led to a surge in support. Well over half the money raised came in the last two weeks of the campaign.

Richmond's plane, called Jubilee, had a rather undistinguished career. To the RAF she was just Spitfire Mk IIIB no P8347. During 1941 she served with 222 Squadron engaged in fighter sweeps across northern France. Within a few months, however, she was mothballed as newer marks of Spitfires were introduced and she was finally scrapped in 1944.[viii]

The Spitfire Fund was the first of many successful appeals. Almost £1,000 was raised at the end of 1941 for various war charities. For example, £100 was sent to Mrs Churchill's Fund for Russia and £104 spent on cigarettes for members of the East Surrey Regiment, the local regiment. After Paddy Finucane's death a Memorial Fund in his name raised £8,000 for the Richmond Royal Hospital. Even this was dwarfed by the Warship Week of 1941, in which £250,000 was raised to adopt HMS *Richmond,* and the Wings for Victory campaign eventually made £460,00 (enough to buy 23 Mosquito aircraft). Betty Coldman, who was involved in several campaigns, remembered that 'we used to push a barrel organ through the streets and along to the Castle Hotel... The GIs were always very generous...they had more money than us anyway and liked to show off to their girls.'[ix]

Morale, News and Rumour

Despite reverses at Dunkirk, Crete and Singapore, and the more immediate terrors of the Blitz, morale among the British remained remarkably high. The thought of defeat never seemed to enter into people's minds. It may be because, unlike the rest of Europe, the British had had no experience of invasion; so the concept was alien. The most common complaints during the dark days of 1940 seem to have been about the lack of sleep because of the raids and moans about the selfishness of other people in air-raid-shelters. In September 1940 the *Thames Valley Times* grumbled:

> Complaints have been made in some quarters near wardens' posts of the over loud talking of wardens who stand about in the open at night when the 'Raiders passed' has sounded and talk over what they have or have not seen. They forget that some people would be glad to go to sleep.[x]

The British government controlled the provision of information, both directly and indirectly. Most people got their news either through the BBC's Home Programme or through daily newspapers. Of these the BBC was the most trusted, because its listeners thought that, by and large, it was telling the truth. Despite wartime restrictions, local newspapers seemed to serve their conservative middle-class readers well, although they were subjected to censorship particularly about the location and effect of raids.

Yet the government could not control what might be called indirect news, particularly rumours which originated from nowhere, spreading like wildfire, which unchecked could seriously affect morale. It was believed that malicious rumours had contributed to the collapse of France during May and June 1940. The authorities were determined that this should not happen here. Indeed it became an offence to spread malicious rumours. In August 1940, Richmond Council set up a network of ward information committees to disseminate information locally in an attempt to prevent rumours, particularly when newspapers and broadcasting had been temporarily suspended. The intention was to post accurate news on noticeboards in each district.[xi]

This machinery was used only twice. In late August 1940, a message was posted on the noticeboard outside the Town Hall on Hill Street:

> A rumour is current in certain parts of the borough to the effect that enemy parachutists have landed in the Old Deer Park and are at

large. This malicious rumour is entirely without foundation and information as to the identity of any person spreading the rumour should be reported to the police.[xii]

A month later there were wide-spread rumours that the Germans had actually landed. If believed, this could have caused panic among the civilian population. On 30 September, it was reported that: 'On instructions from headquarters a notice was placed outside the Town Hall on Wednesday evening stating that rumours that there had been an invasion at Dover or anywhere else in the British Isles were untrue.'[xiii]

Inevitably people became weary of the war and its privations. Despite constant reminders they forgot their gas masks and ignored air-raid warnings. They used the black market to buy little luxuries and had more than their fair share of hot water. As the bad news piled up they also lost enthusiasm for the war itself.

Lieutenant Stephen Paull of the US Army had noted this dour attitude as early as 1941, when he found that even a major event like the Japanese attack on Pearl Harbor did not move the drinkers at the Roebuck on Richmond Hill: 'A few people casually remarked to us that "they guessed we were in it now too". English people do not get greatly excited over seemingly important news. Perhaps two years of war has made them that way.'[xiv]

For two more years they were still more dour. The war appeared to have drifted into a stalemate, with neither Allies nor the Axis apparently able to deliver a knock-out blow.

[i] Museum of Richmond, *Catalogue for Richmond at War: the Civilian Experience 1939-45* (Museum of Richmond, 1992), p12.

[ii] Ibid, p13; Leach, John, *Richmond Shop Boy's War* (RLHS, 2005), p15.

[iii] Museum of Richmond, *Catalogue for Richmond at War: the Civilian Experience 1939-45* (Museum of Richmond, 1992), p27.

[iv] *Richmond and Twickenham Times*, 6 March 1943. It was possible to have a take-away so long as you provided your own dixie or container.

[v] Much of this page is based on a WVS blog at www.royalvoluntaryservice.org.uk/about-us/our-history/wrvs-archive-and-heritage-collection/heritage-bulletin-blog.

[vi] This paragraph is based on a note prepared by Laurence Bain: 'The History of Fences during World War 2 1939 -1945' for the Friends of Richmond Green.

[vii] For more about Finucane and Richmond, see www.stmgrts.org.uk/archives/2011/06/spitfire_paddy.html
Leach, John, *Richmond Shop Boy's War* (RLHS, 2005).

[viii] See the article at www.richmondhistory.org.uk/wordpress/history-of-richmond/richmond-at-war. There are scrapbooks at Richmond Local Studies Library. For Jubilee, see http://spitfiresite.com/2010/04/presentation-spitfires.html.

[ix] Museum of Richmond, *Catalogue for Richmond at War: the Civilian Experience 1939-45* (Museum of Richmond, 1992), pp9, 26. HMS *Richmond* was originally an old American destroyer USS *Fairfax*, which was taken over by the Royal Navy in 1941 and used to escort convoys across the Atlantic. She was sold to the Soviet Navy in 1944 and finally broken up in 1949 (see her Wikipedia entry).

[x] *Thames Valley Times,* 14 September 1940. The Ministry of Information conducted daily surveys of morale, see Addison, Paul, and Craig, James, *Listening To Britain: Home Intelligence Reports on Britain's Finest Hour* (Vintage, 2011), which includes several mentions of Richmond. The reports themselves are at the National Archives in series INF 1, with additional material at the Imperial War Museum.

[xi] A Dutch Jesuit priest, Father Houben of Cheam, was fined £10 at Richmond Magistrates Court for 'making statements to Belgian refugees likely to cause alarm and despondency.' *The Times*, 26 July 1940.
Richmond and Twickenham Times, 22 August 1940.

[xii] *Richmond and Twickenham Times*, 31 August 1940. The 29th and 30th saw a number of dog fights and air-raid alarms over the town which may have led to the rumour.

[xiii] *Richmond and Twickenham Times,* 30 September 1940. Marie Lawrence noted in her diary for 16 September that 'Today is the day of the invasion', but it did not affect her routine, as she was much keener to record that she had received a prize for her shorthand at the local commercial college.

[xiv] Stephen Paull papers, diary entry 7 December 1941, Imperial War Museum.

CHAPTER 6 – *Doodlebug Summer*

On 12 June 1944 the Germans began sending unmanned rockets against Britain. Their launch was in retaliation to the Allied invasion of Normandy that had occurred a few days earlier. There were two versions – the V1, nicknamed the Doodlebug or Buzzbomb, and the V2, a guided ballistic missile. Just under ten thousand V1s were launched against London and the South East during the summer and autumn of 1944, followed by a few hundred V2 rockets. These devices were potentially devastating but, although they did cause great damage, their effect was much reduced, as most V1s were destroyed by gunfire or fighter planes before they reached their targets. However, it was impossible to shoot down V2s as they travelled at twice the speed of sound.[i]

Richmond's first V1 arrived on 19 June. According to the *Richmond Herald*, it landed 'in the allotments in Old Deer Park and damage was done to a hundred properties, not one seriously. Many were attracted to the scene of the incident, but there was not much for them to see, and the nearby crops appeared to have been slightly damaged.'[ii]

This, however, was just the first of what appeared to many local people to be an armada directed straight at the heart of Richmond. Marie Lawrence wrote in her diary for 19 June:

> The blessed things just came over and we listen for the engine to stop. Several times right over our heads. Until at last really felt we could stand it no more. So many for sure had our name on it. Dad would keep looking out until I was hysterical. At last he suggested we went to the public shelter as he thought we were in the line of fire. It sounded like it and with darkness all around we could not see… We were up all night and still at 6 and 6.30 more planes were still coming in. Dad got himself ready for work and left. Explosion after explosion went off and at about 8.30 we threw ourselves down in the passage as the front door rattled. Found after it was a big one on Twickenham Junction and some people were killed… Everyone looks miserable.

Peter Horrocks, who was training with the Phantom Regiment in Richmond Park, was equally alarmed:

> Our officers' mess [Pembroke Lodge] was on the edge of the ridge above the Thames and…provided a good view of those missiles, which had not been shot down on the final stages of

their journey to central London; they seemed to be almost at eye-level, at varying distances away from us.

While you could hear their engine running they were no danger; someone else would get the impact. One incident I remember clearly. It was on a Sunday morning, a lovely fine day, and a group of us was standing outside enjoying a pre-lunch drink while we watched this aerial show – the bombs flying in and anti-aircraft fire attempting to bring them down. Suddenly the engine of one of the bombs, which was quite close and clearly visible, spluttered to a stop and the bomb's flight immediately started to curve downwards.

I cannot now remember how many of us were there but I do recall that, with one accord, every one of us went inside through the French windows and finished up in an undignified heap between two large sofas placed back to back in the middle of the room. Without a word or any pre-planning all of us had the same instinct of self-preservation and in the same moment worked out the same route to safety without any consideration of the hierarchy of rank. There were some crumpled uniforms, some spilt drinks and broken glasses as we untangled ourselves from the makeshift shelter to resume our drinking, chatter and, in due course lunch.[iii]

The civil authorities had little idea about how to cope with the new threat. Indeed there was little they could do. Because the arrival of these missiles was entirely random, it was impossible to organise any effective form of protection. Nine-year-old Roy Featherstone was taught that if the engine stopped you must throw yourself on the ground and cover your head with your hands. 'I am not sure,' he added wryly, 'what it would achieve if it landed near or on you.'[iv]

The numbers of people using the public shelters increased from nil in March and April 1944 to 3,000 a night in June and July.[v]

During the period of the V1 menace many children were sent north to the industrial towns of Lancashire and Yorkshire. The Council received official approval to declare Richmond an evacuation zone to allow the evacuation of children and their mothers on 8 July. Within a week 558 unaccompanied children and 722 expectant mothers or mothers with children had been registered.

Evacuation began on the 13th. Eventually 922 children and mothers left the town. Unaccompanied children were escorted by their teachers while the others were led by 'public spirited ladies'. One of the councillors who took a party to Leeds described the arrangements as being 'marvellous'. Inevitably there was a slow drift back home in the late summer as the V1 raids came to an end.

A section from the National Fire Service outside the main fire station on Shaftesbury Road in 1944

Walter d'Hondt's house on Queen's Road was one of those badly damaged by a V1 explosion: 'My mother and sister and I went to Codds Farm in Holm (near Bath) where I spent a memorable number of months riding a horse that was close to being sent to the glue factory, and milking cows, taking care of the sheep, ducks and chickens, and digging up potatoes.'[vi]

Harold Gray wrote in the *Richmond Parish Magazine*:

> Most of our children are away, less than fifty are left in our Day School, the rest have gone to so many places, and to all the hospitable people who are entertaining them we are very grateful for the welcome they have given them and the care they are taking of them. Our Headmaster took a party of 150, some of them our own children, to Burnley...[vii]

The speed of the rockets meant that it was almost impossible to find safety. Marie Lawrence, who had survived several close shaves during the Blitz, noted in her diary on 17 June: 'Night is now falling and I feel nervous about it.' Eventually she went to see her doctor who recommended an over-the-counter nerve tonic.

Richmond was fortunately spared the loss of life that the V1 wrought on other places, but many buildings were damaged.[*] The worst incident occurred at midnight on 27 June when a bomb landed in the Thames just upstream from Richmond Bridge:

> Extensive damage was done to property on both sides of the river and in the centre of Richmond few windows were intact.... When daylight came it seemed as if the town had been struck by a tornado.[viii]

Jenny Oliver's father-in-law Richard was an unwilling observer of this V1's descent:

> [He] was cycling over Richmond Bridge to get news of the latest invasion, when a doodlebug came over stopping just above the bridge. He stared at it and in his fright put his brakes on hard. He went over the top of his handlebars, landing hard on the floor and cutting his chin. Bike and Dick sat waiting on the floor but luckily the doodlebug caused very little damage to the bridge. Dick got up, checked his bike and went on to get news of the invasion. It was not until he got home that he realised how lucky he had been.[**][ix]

Marie Lawrence wrote:

> 12.15 another bang. Woke up to all clear and then sirens and bangs. When I got to Martin's shop he said 'You will have something to look at' I said not the Plot again. 'No', he replied 'one landed near the Pigeons'. [***] I said I was astonished and he banged me on the back and said 'Don't look so bad about it.' When I got to the bridge the glass was out of all the shops and

---

[*] There were, however, two deaths in Kew. See Blomfield, David, and May, Christopher, *Kew at War* (RLHS, 2009) p 48.

[**] The *Richmond and Twickenham Times* of 9 September 1944 reported that 'for days after the river was full of dead fish'.

[***] The Pigeons, or Three Pigeons, was a popular riverside pub on the site of Richmond Canoe Club.

Strathmore Hotel was blown in and out...The nearer I got to Langholm Lodge the less the blast was on the houses but in the dip in Petersham Road the houses were very blown about.[x]

Other incidents of note occurred on 23 July when a bomb landed in the grounds of the Methodist College at the top of Queen's Road (now the American International University) and a month later on 23 August when Old Palace Lane was hit.

The real damage, however, was psychological. Leoni Burke says that she was 'more frightened of doodlebugs than of the aircraft and other bombs, and used to hold her breath wondering where they were going to drop.' Many people remembered for the rest of their lives the distinct throbbing noise that the V1 made followed by an eerie silence and then a few seconds later an almighty explosion. Mike Evans says that, even after 70 years, 'that sound still haunts me – as I have found it does others.'[xi]

[i] Only two V2s landed in the borough, one in Richmond Park, and the other at the Chrysler works in Kew on 19 September 1944, where seven men were killed, as described in *Kew at War* (RLHS 2009). The blast destroyed eight houses in West Park Avenue, with a death toll of a further six.

[ii] *Richmond Herald*, 5 January 1946.

[iii] Peter Horrocks contribution to the BBC People's War Project www.bbc.co.uk/history/ww2peopleswar/stories/13/a3830113.shtml.

[iv] Featherstone, Roy, 'Memories of Kew in WW2'.

[v] Richmond Council minutes, 18 July 1944.

[vi] Report of Civil Defence Committee, 18 July 1944.

Walter d'Hondt email to Local History Society, 20 August 2013.

[vii] *Richmond Parish Magazine*, July 1944.

[viii] *Richmond Herald*, 5 January 1946.

[ix] Pat Oakely contribution to the BBC People's War Project: www.bbc.co.uk/history/ww2peopleswar/stories/72/a4699272.shtml.

[x] Marie Lawrence's diary, 27 June 1944.

[xi] Mike Evans email to author.

Leonie Burke interview with Alette Anderson, 23 June 2013.

CHAPTER 7 – *Work and Volunteering*

The need for labour for the war effort permeated British society from dowager to dinner lady, school child to retiree. Everybody was expected to contribute and if this was not forthcoming the state could compel individuals to participate. Men and women between the ages of 18 and 42 were conscripted. Most men joined the armed forces, but from December 1943 an unlucky ten per cent became Bevin Boys working in coal mines. Individuals could nominate the service they wished to serve in: the RAF was by far the most popular choice and they had the pick of the men to choose from. However, skilled men, who it was thought would contribute more to the war by remaining outside the forces, were placed in reserved occupations and so were not subject to call up. Men were also expected to volunteer for the Home Guard, as air-raid wardens or in various other ways.

For the first time women were also conscripted. Most were directed to working in factories. There was little heavy industry in Richmond, although there was the Hawker works on the Kingston/Ham border and Chrysler in Kew, which employed hundreds of local women (and some men). But some preferred to go into the forces or joined the Land Army that helped on the land. As a result local girls found themselves in many positions that would have been inconceivable before the war. Lorna Hawley, for example, was sent to the Naval Signal Office based in the caves under Dover Castle where she found the work 'intensely interesting, though it entailed all-night duty every third night'. Muriel Glass initially worked in the Photographic Library at the Ministry Of Information before being sent to the Middle East Coordinating Centre in Cairo as an establishment (personnel) officer: 'She loved the Middle East despite the incessant bouts of illness.' Lorna Manley was awarded an MBE for her work at the British Embassy in Athens in 1944. Margaret Scudamore commented that: 'For my part our hair rose to such an extent when we heard a few of her experiences that we thought this absurdly inadequate.'[i]

Women also volunteered for civil defence work, joined the Women's Voluntary Service (WVS) or helped with knitting parties making comforts for the troops. During 1942 a group of volunteers at Eton Lodge on Paradise Road knitted 272 garments 'pullovers, cap mufflers, scarves, mufflers, gloves and helmets etc' for men in the Navy, RAF and Red

Army. In addition, girls at the County School knitted items for the Merchant Navy and Royal Navy, as well as gloves for the Russians.[ii]

There were also a number of women's auxiliaries in the Home Guard. Richmond was one of the first battalions to recruit women. Initially there were 120 lady volunteers: 'And very smart they looked in their uniforms of khaki overalls, with armband on which was painted in green Women's Auxiliary Section.' They trained in first aid and signalling, did clerical work and took messages between the sections scattered across the borough. 'The Canteen Section fed us and, what is more they washed up after we had eaten; and they all smiled and looked charming throughout.'[iii]

Parade of the women members of the Auxiliary Fire Service in the Lower Mortlake Road

The fact that so many local men and women were in uniform or away on war work led to severe problems locally. Those remaining at home had to cover for those who had been called up. A particular problem was a perennial shortage of labour to dig new shelters and to shore-up and repair bomb-damaged buildings. The Air Raid Precautions organisation depended largely on volunteers, as to an extent did the police and fire services. Eighteen-year-old Daphne Harris recalled that she was perhaps not an ideal recruit:

I heard that Richmond ARP needed drivers and [Ambulance] Attendants so I joined them. My driving experience was six half-hour lessons after which I was asked to drive through Ealing Broadway and I had, it seemed, passed the test... I was given a left-hand drive Packard which had been converted into an ambulance. It seemed enormous to me. I was given a test run in daylight following the stretcher car and everyone seemed happy about my performance. I was not so sanguine! I drove at night once with no lights, and then there was an SOS for Attendants. So conscious of my inexperience compared to the other drivers I volunteered to be an Attendant.

I was sent up to the Star and Garter Home for lessons in First Aid. I passed the Test more by luck than judgement and there I was an Attendant with a great deal of enthusiasm, but very little knowledge.

Teenagers too were expected to contribute. Many boys joined the Army Cadets, Sea Cadets or Air Training Corps, which provided some basic training and a flavour of what life was like in the services. In 1940, Stan Knight, then aged fourteen, joined Richmond Sea Cadets, which were based in what had once been the Compasses Hotel on Petersham Road. It was commanded by Ward Edgecombe March who 'possessed a tremendous teaching ability and was able to train his cadets [in] all the qualities, skills and disciplines required if they were in time to serve aboard a ship.' Their duties included guarding a building used by the Admiralty in the town.[iv]

Conscientious Objectors

After the introduction of conscription in the First World War there grew up the phenomenon of the Conscientious Objector – men who for religious or political reasons refused to undertake military service. The authorities found it very hard to cope with such men, who often suffered badly for their beliefs. During the Second World War this was not so great a problem. In part this was because the War was clearly a fight against evil, but also because the rights of objectors were recognised by the government. However, it was expected that individual objectors should serve in some non-combatant capacity, notably either in Civil Defence or working on the land. Even so there were a few individuals for whom this compromise was too much. They were opposed to war in all its forms.

In Richmond opposition to military service centred on the Fellowship of Conscientious Objectors, which had emerged from several smaller groups in 1937. The Fellowship was perhaps at its most influential in the early days of the war, when it organised several meetings for young men who did not want to enlist, and handed out leaflets at the Labour Exchange at Onslow Hall on Little Green where men registered to serve. On 8 March 1940 forty members of the group handed out leaflets to new recruits before being roughly manhandled by the police. Later, detectives visited the homes of the Fellowship's officers.[v]

Things changed after Dunkirk. By 1943 the Fellowship was tolerated with a small nucleus of supporters locally. *Peace News* sold about a hundred copies in and around Richmond, and there were regular social events. The writer Vera Brittain chaired a musical evening at the Vineyard Congregational Hall in March 1943, which was attended by fifty to sixty people. A collection of £6 19s was divided between the Food Relief Committee and War Resisters International.

Members of the Fellowship were split in their reactions to conscription. Some accepted the alternatives offered by the government. Stanley Toye, for example, was exempted from the military provided he engaged in forestry work or joined the merchant marine.

Others took a harder line. The Fellowship's secretary and driving force was Charles Fisher who had been a 'Conchie' during the last months of the First World War. Mr Fisher endured a number of prison sentences for his beliefs. In early 1943, for example, he was jailed for two months for failing to appear before a Labour Exchange. The Literature Secretary, John Horton, was sentenced to six months hard labour by Richmond Magistrates Court in May 1943 for refusing to take up land or Civil Defence work.

[i] Scudamore, Margaret, *The Richmond and East Sheen County School for Girls: a record 1861-1947* (Richmond, 1947), pp17, 53-54. The book has a list of old girls, summarizing their war service. Unfortunately there is no equivalent for boys.

[ii] Council for Social Service Annual Report, 1942, in Piper Collection Vol 8, p21. Scudamore, p41.

[iii] Redfern, A E, *Reminiscences of the 63rd Surrey (Richmond) Battalion Home Guard* (Richmond, [1946]), pp19-20.

[iv] Knight, Stanley, *Memoirs* (typescript copy), pp1-2.

[v] This section is based largely on a typescript in the Richmond Local Studies Library on the Richmond Pacifist Movement by D E Fisher.

CHAPTER 8 – *Schooling under the Planes*

For many children, the war offered freedoms and excitement that would have been missing in peacetime. Audrey Blackburn, who was about ten when war broke out, recalled:

> Life in wartime for a child living in or near London was a mixture of normality, adventure and danger. We enjoyed a freedom to roam undreamt of by children [today]. The country was bursting with servicemen, both British and foreign, and refugees from overseas, as well as the possibility of 'booby traps' against civilians – articles designed to look innocent but in fact explosive – of which we were constantly warned. But we would spend all day in the few still-open museums in South Kensington or rowing a dinghy on the Thames, or 'tracking' in what remained of Richmond Park.[i]

Roy Featherstone remembered the bombsite on what was once Bartons drapers store, opposite Richmond station:

> We boys, when arriving at the station bus stop, used to dash across the road and onto the bombsite, or what was left of it. Half way across was a drop in level of about 3 feet, which we always jumped over at speed, only to be castigated by elderly folk – 'very dangerous' and rush off to the baths.[ii]

Most children seem to have collected pieces of shrapnel. Elsie Erlebach, who was then ten years old, wrote, 'On the way to school each day we would collect shrapnel…The most gruesome pieces were admired.'[iii]

The more adventurous collected live ammunition. Walter d'Hondt who lived on Richmond Hill would 'occasionally go through the fence in our garden and explore the hotel garden, which was under disrepair, where I found the ammunition of the troops that were barracked there at the back of the hotel. I would take the ammunition and trade it at school for banana and orange peels, because given rationing I didn't realize there was more to the fruits than that, and I valued them greatly.'[iv]

Air-raid wardens would regularly come to talk to the children telling them to avoid picking up unexploded bombs. Mike Evans's memories of his primary school in East Sheen included:

> Air-raid wardens talking to the school more than once…on one occasion they brought in the fin off a bomb and told us how it was

designed to 'scream' as it fell and so frighten the population below. On another, they warned us about 'Butterfly bombs' and 'Chocolate bombs'. We were told not to touch anything like these – but to report finding any to adults.[v]

Even gas masks had their attractions. Jenny Webb remembers: 'I used to like to put it on, and blow hard at the little hole in the front, to make the nose blow up and waggle, and make a rude noise!'[vi]

The downside was that unsupervised children could be accused of vandalising the shelters, which must have been a tempting target. In November 1940 the *Richmond Herald* complained that 'the authorities have not been helped either, by damage done to the group shelters by children. A bill of £16 has just been met dealing with damage in one area. Rubbish has been found piled in the shelters and bricks torn away by the emergency exits.' [vii]

Evacuation

On the outbreak of war there was no formal evacuation of local children to safer areas, as happened in Inner London and other large cities. Nor did Richmond become a reception area for evacuees. Instead the Borough was in what the Home Office called a neutral area, which meant that individual parents could send children to safer areas, or even overseas if they so wished. About 100 girls from the County School for Girls out of an enrolment of 380 did not start in September 1939 and, although many trickled back during the Phoney War, the start of the Blitz sent their numbers up again.[viii]

Things were similar at the new County School for Boys in East Sheen, although here matters were complicated by the fact that the autumn term of 1939 saw the merger of the Richmond and East Sheen schools on one site. John Leach, who was a pupil at the school, thought that some of the evacuated boys took advantage of the inevitable chaos and 'were never seen again by their classmates and I am not sure if the new school knew where they were either.'[ix]

After their house in Peldon Avenue had been destroyed in September 1940, Audrey Blackburn and her twin brother were sent to distant relations in Yorkshire: 'We didn't know them and they didn't know us, and although the lady did her best to cope with two young children we both felt very homesick and everything around us was totally unfamiliar.' They eventually returned to a new home in Queen's Road in August the following year.[x]

Even so there were several petitions from local residents calling upon the Council to organise children's evacuation. In November 1940 the Council resolved that:

> the Ministry of Health be informed that the council have received a petition from a large number of residents and the Council again request the Minister to extend to Richmond the facilities which apply in certain other parts of London for the voluntary evacuation of women and children.

The Ministry declined to take action, possibly because it was receiving too many similar appeals by other councils, and to agree would have swamped existing arrangements.[xi]

However, as we have seen, nearly a thousand children were evacuated to Lancashire and Yorkshire with the arrival of the V1s and V2s during the summer of 1944.[xii]

Evacuated children and their parents being welcomed by the Mayor of Leeds, July 1944

Education

Children's education was severely affected by the Blitz. It is something that the children themselves often did not realise. As we have seen, memoirs and oral history accounts tend to dwell on other aspects of the war, such as collecting shrapnel, the experience of air-raid shelters, or the absence of fathers on military service. However, air raids led to serious dislocation of the school system. They also affected the children themselves because the alarms and the raids affected their daily routines and the hours they could sleep.

Mr W H Lugg, headmaster of St John's School, reported:
> The younger children were much less sleepy than the older ones, probably because they are taken down to the shelters asleep and stay there in happy oblivion, while the older ones remain alert during the raid. Even at play the children were much less lively and noisy, while most teachers found them 'slow in the uptake' and have given them easier lessons.[xiii]

Mary Buck, who attended Darell Road School, had a great deal of sympathy for the head teacher:
> The Headmaster was a man called George Lester and what a responsibility he had. He had to deal with children who were often tired through lack of sleep, children who were missing their fathers, and so much more, plus when the V1 rockets came the responsibility of getting all the children into the shelters and often keeping them there all day.[xiv]

Miss Horn, who taught at the County School for Girls, summed up the teacher's role:
> We tried to think of every possible emergency so that we should not fail the [girls]. We hope that the absence of panic or hysteria at any time was a testimony to the thoroughness of our preparations. For we worked hard to make them feel as safe as possible in such trying circumstances.[xv]

Schools lost teachers who were called up or were absent as the result of raids. Buildings were damaged. But the worst problem facing teachers was that lessons were continually being disrupted by warnings, which meant that it was very hard for either staff or their classes to concentrate. Mary Buck recalled 'the huge amount of time we spent in the shelters in North Sheen Recreation Ground'.

The school logbook for the Central Boys School in Gainsborough Road, Kew, recorded on 29 September 1940:

> At 11am violent gunfire of an enemy plane could be heard overhead. Boys sheltered immediately in corridor (no siren) returning to normal at 11.30am. Siren warning at 11.45-12.20, then 12.25-12.55. Afternoon school 2.15 start. Siren 3.10-3.47.[xvi]

On 25 October the school logbook for the County School for Girls in Parkshot has the following entry:

> 8.50-10.45 Enemy plane so low over the school. The markings were visible. The sirens went again at a minute to twelve midday while all the children were still in school. It is now 3.30 and the raid is still on. Some parents have taken the children away, but the majority are still here. All have eaten their iron rations, all the milk has been drunk and many Horlicks tablets consumed. All clear ten minutes to four.[xvii]

At the Girls' school each shelter had room for two classes:

> The mistresses taking lessons found it easiest to teach standing back to back in the middle so that their voices travelled in opposite directions and as little as possible confused one another's classes. But it was very difficult because, as they did their work, the voices of the girls rang back from the close-set walls.[xviii]

However dedicated the teachers, it would have been very difficult to learn anything in the dark, chilly and often damp shelters. And the smaller children, who might have been very scared, must have needed considerable reassurance. Mike Evans, who attended East Sheen Primary School, remembered that 'I only recall going into the air-raid shelters…once. We seemed to sit there forever and Miss Hughes had us all singing, "Lay that pistol down ma, lay that pistol down. Pistol packing mama, lay that pistol down!"'.[xix]

Children inevitably got thirsty and hungry or wanted to go to the loo. At Parkshot:

> Great pottery jugs were put near the entrance to each shelter with a tin plate on top to keep dust out, and with a tin mug on top from which to drink. The crates of milk bottles had to be brought over at break time. Dinners had to be taken on trolleys from the exit door of the dining room, round the gravel path, across the playground and through the doors in the wall to shelter tops. After

the mid-day meal small groups of girls in turn had to be conducted to the lavatories in the lulls.[xx]

One is full of admiration for teachers who kept the schools going under considerable difficulty, while still managing to teach and nurture their charges. School leaving examinations at the County School for Girls were affected by the uncertainty, here described by Margaret Scudamore at the time of the doodlebug attacks:

> The Higher School candidates were set up in one of the shelters, and their examinations proceeded without interruption. But there were far too many General School candidates for similar arrangements to be made for them. They had to be dispersed in two long rows from end to end of the lower corridor. I sat on the front steps facing up into the direction from which the doodlebugs came. The sound of the siren and the arrival of the bomb were almost simultaneous, at which moment I gave the word to down pens and make for the shelters. There the girls had to sit without talking... One three-hour paper was interrupted six or seven times.[*][xxi]

Members of 217 Squadron Women's Junior Air Corps

---

[*] Higher Examinations were equivalent to A-Levels and General Examinations to O-Levels or the GCSE.

[i]   Audrey Blackburn contribution to BBC People's War Project
www.bbc.co.uk/history/ww2peopleswar/stories/56/a6314456.shtml.

[ii]   Featherstone, Roy, *Memories of Kew in WW2*.

[iii]   Letter to Richmond Local History Society, 20 May 2013.

[iv]   Email from Walter d'Hondt to Richmond Local History Society, 20 August 2013.

[v]   Email from Mike Evans to author, 8 March 2015.

[vi]   Museum of Richmond, *Catalogue for Richmond at War: the Civilian Experience 1939-45* (Museum of Richmond, 1992), p6.

[vii]   *Richmond Herald*, 29 November 1940. See complaints about vandalism to the doors of Town Hall shelter, 17 October 1940 TNA HO 207/988. See also the letter from Mr J D Allinson complaining about vandalism to the doors of Town Hall shelter, 17 October 1940 TNA HO 207/988.

[viii] Scudamore, Margaret, *The Richmond and East Sheen County School for Girls: a record 1861-1947* (Richmond, 1947), pp28-9.

[ix]   Leach, John, *Richmond Shop Boy's War* (RLHS, 2006), p4.

[x]   Scudamore, Margaret, *The Richmond and East Sheen County School for Girls: a record 1861-1947* (Richmond, 1947), pp28-9.
Audrey Blackburn contribution to BBC People's War Project
www.bbc.co.uk/history/ww2peopleswar/stories/56/a6314456.shtml

[xi]   Emergency Committee, 9 November 1940.

[xii]   See Chapter 6.

[xiii]   *Richmond Herald*, 29 November 1940. Adults were also affected by the lack of sleep. Marie Lawrence's diaries, for example, are full of grumbles about her sleeping badly because of the raids.

[xiv]   Email from Mary Buck to the author, 9 June 2014.

[xv]   Quoted in Scudamore, p38.

[xvi]   School Log Book Richmond County School for Boys, 29 September 1940, pp112-113. School logs offer a good source for the exact timings of raids and alerts.

[xvii]   School Log Book Richmond County School for Girls, 25 October 1940, p94.

[xviii] Scudamore, p30.

[xix]   Mike Evans email, 8 March 2015.

[xx]   Scudamore, p30.

[xxi]   Scudamore, pp31-32.

CHAPTER 9 – *Pleasure and Leisure*

It was possible to escape the war in various ways. Indeed for most people it became essential. The most popular form of entertainment was the cinema – Richmond alone had four cinemas: the Premier (now the Odeon), the Royalty, the Ritz and the Electric (the Curzon cinema is on its site). Here patrons could sit in the warm dark and enjoy programmes of escapist but uplifting feature films, newsreels and shorter items, such as cartoons and appeals from local dignitaries to help with some aspect of the war effort. All this for a shilling or two. Cinema-going nationally reached a peak during the War with 1.5 billion visits alone in 1944, and Richmond was no exception to this.[i]

Richmond Theatre, on the Green, continued to put on an array of plays. In May 1943 the attractions included a long-forgotten farce *The Family Upstairs* about a middle class family in Manhattan. [ii]

There were a number of churches and a synagogue in the town, which continued to minister to parishioners, despite bomb damage and the other privations of war. (St Matthias church was particularly badly damaged.) As well as services, they organised social and fund-raising events, and most kept in touch with members in the forces, sending regular newsletters.

The Church also played a full part in the debates about creating a better world as well as a better Richmond. In June 1943, for example, the town's churches organised a 'Religion and Life Week' to discuss among other issues:

> Is the coming victory to end war between civilised men, or is it to prepare the way for the next? Are there again to be millions of unemployed in our land? Are good homes and good education to be the privilege of the few? What about the backward races and countries where poverty is widespread? How can we improve our community life, our opportunities for fellowship, for recreation, for culture, for leisure and the good use of it?

The town had always been something of a holiday spot, particularly for day-trippers from London, visiting Kew Gardens, the Riverside and Richmond Park. This became even more important in wartime, when many seaside resorts, like Margate and Brighton, were out of bounds to civilians. Because the town was relatively unscathed it became a particularly important oasis for Londoners. A local naval rating Stan Knight remembers:

> Richmond was a lively town, people still crowded there for a good time, the pubs and the various cafes, and streets full of service men of all ranks and nationalities enjoying their leave... When on leave we used to drink in the Victoria on Hill Rise... and playing snooker in the White Cross pub by the river, sometimes hearing at night, when an air raid was on, shrapnel from anti-aircraft shells snapping into the water. And also a few jolly evenings up on the Richmond Terrace with some of the lovely Surrey girls, our uniform still had a bit of magic in those days.[iii]

The pubs were never busier than during the war years, although the beer was weak and supplies often limited. Another local resident, John Wright, remembered: 'In the evening The Ship, and a good many other pubs, would be crammed to the doors with servicemen and, by spring 1942, with a strong American presence.'[iv]

One of the first GIs to arrive in the town, Stephen Paull, described the Roebuck on Richmond Hill as it was in November 1941:

> People cluster there of a Sunday morning and discuss the adventures of the previous evening over a mug of Scotch ale: 'I say did you get home alright last night etc'. It is so crowded in there one can hardly elbow his way to the bar for a drink. Avoiding spilling the ale is an accomplishment.[v]

Probably the most popular pub was the Castle Hotel by the Town Hall, where locals and soldiers happily rubbed shoulders. John Wright remembered it as being 'notorious'. Now long demolished it was a rather rambling building where there was also a ballroom where regular dances with Bob Garganido and his Band were held on Wednesday evenings.[vi]

Troops in Richmond

Richmond became quite a centre for service personnel. In December 1941 Lieutenant Stephen Paull mused:

> The section of Richmond near the park appears to be an ordinary residential section of old houses and apartment hotels. To look at them would reveal nothing. But actually they are radio schools, offices, workshops, troop barracks and radio control positions.

Clearly these are 'military objectives' – if knowledge of this condition got into enemy hands.[vii]

In particular, there were concentrations of troops in Richmond Park (see Chapter 10). There were also several American units, notably the cartographic draftsmen in Kew, and small numbers elsewhere in the borough. The first group, including Lt Paull, arrived to train at the secret radar school in Petersham in October 1941. This was before the United States formally entered the War.

Across the river the Allied Supreme Commander, General Dwight D Eisenhower, had his headquarters in Bushy Park and many men based there must have come to Richmond on their days and nights off.

Inevitably, links grew up between these men and the local community. Some were formal. The local Council of Social Service, for example, supported an American Red Cross club for US Troops at Trumpeters' House on Richmond Green, which provided facilities for homesick GIs. A highlight was a party organised by the Club for 300 local children whose fathers were away fighting, or prisoners of war or who had been during the war. Mary Buck remembers being disappointed that she had not been invited because her father had just been invalided out of the Army.[viii]

Most contacts, however, were informal. Servicemen made friends at church or in the pubs and cafés. Americans and Canadians found themselves invited to local homes for a meal. Betty Coldman remembered that 'my family often invited American servicemen to dinner. We found them charming and polite. They often brought food with them, that could not be obtained on the rations…When the GIs left the area Richmond seemed dead without them.'[ix]

Of the British troops, the Phantom Regiment, with their headquarters at Pembroke Lodge, probably made the most impact on the town. Betty Watts's first boyfriend was 'Brian' a private in the regiment. Men socialised in pubs – the Lass of Richmond Hill was a particular favourite – and it was a common sight to see officers dashing up Richmond Hill from the station to meet a strictly enforced curfew of midnight.

During the spring of 1941 several entertainments were organised by the Regiment at which some of the top stars of the time appeared. It helped

March 19, 1982

Philip Warner Esq

The White Cottage
21 Heatherdale Road
CAMBERLEY, Surrey GU15 2LT

Dear Mr. Warner, (Philip)

Forgive rush, I'm catching a plane for California.

Yes, it is true. When 'A' squadron was doing intensive training around ~~handle~~
Dartmoor I did answer an SOS from the Navy who were trying to ~~cope with~~ handle
E-boats which had twin Oerlikons pooping off from an armour-plated bridge
and all they had was 3-pounder salute guns off, I suppose, the Victory or
something like that with which to cope. Anyway, they had their eyes on
our anti-tank rifles so I called for volunteers hoping nobody would suggest
that I went too but unfortunately everybody wanted to have a few nights at
sea so off we went but, thank God, apart from endemic sea-sickness and the
squadron's cook losing his teeth overboard nothing happened. No E-boats
showed up or if they did, thank God nobody noticed them.

The other saga was the pigeon. Hoppy gave us baskets of these foul beasts
to carry messages when all else failed. I think General Paget was the
Commander-in-Chief Home Forces and an elaborate loft was constructed outside
his headquarters, ~~I believe~~ in St. James's Park. Hoppy told him with great
pride that messages would soon be arriving from the far-flung squadrons.
Paget waited expectantly and at last a bird slapped in through the intake
box. It was from 'A' squadron. A massive exercise was in progress all over
southern England and the message was ripped off the poor bird's leg and read
in expectant hush as follows: "That beast Major Niven sent me away because
he said I had farted in the nest". I understand there was not much happy
laughter in St. James's Park!

I have forgotten the name of the Scandinavian actress I brought to the Richmond
party who pinched everybody's cap badges but I do remember organizing a concert
in Richmond for the entire outfit which included Flannigan and Allen, Nervo
and Nox, Frances Day, Zoe Gale, Norton and Gold, Teddy Brown and his xylophone,
Naunton Wayne, Arthur Riscoe, Lesley Hanson and Debroy Sommers and his entire
band. I believe the show was a hit though as master of ceremonies I was too
drunk to be able to assess it properly and afterwards, in the officers mess,
one of the Crazy Gang asked Hoppy what the sandwiches had inside them. Hoppy
pointed to a flag on the pile marked 'sardine'. Whereupon Jimmy Nervo, ~~I
think it was~~, ate the flag, brushed the sardine sandwiches to the floor and
broke the plate on Hoppy's head.

They were wonderful days which I would not have missed for anything.

All good wishes, David N.

**Letter from David Niven,
recalling the show he organised for the Phantom Regiment**

71

that the matinée idol David Niven was commander of A Squadron. The highlight was undoubtedly the late night concert at the Premier Cinema (now the Odeon) on 27 May 1941. It followed the regimental sports day in the Old Deer Park:

> A whole fleet of transport brought stardom to its stage door. There was Debroy Somers complete with band, most of the Crazy Gang, Leslie Hanson, Arthur Riscoe and others. The Scottish officers of the Regiment had themselves and their wives piped into the hall. The subsequent party in the Mess beggared belief. Their admirers would have given much to have seen Flanagan and Allen performing one of the more complicated forms of Highland Dance in the hall...[x]

David Niven said that 'the show lasted for four hours and was wildly appreciated', although he later confessed that 'as master of ceremonies, I was too drunk to be able to assess it properly.' [xi]

Along the river

Although welcome, visitors presented an unusual problem because in the case of an air raid it was not possible to protect everybody, particularly on a fine summer's day – and 1940 was one of the best summers of the twentieth century. After considering the matter the Council decided they could do very little to protect the trippers.[xii]

The throngs of visitors concerned a local resident W B Currell who wrote to the Ministry of Home Security:

> I wish to point out how a further danger of such masses of people being congested where there is insufficient shelter for them and that is a military one. I suggest most respectfully that the roads, bridges and streets will be blocked by undisciplined civilians and that the police. ARP personnel, Home Guard would be practically powerless to effect the situation quickly. I am not inferring that there would be a panic, but...[xiii]

In response the Ministry's military liaison officer Captain E Hamilton urged caution:

> ...the only real danger is low flying aeroplanes; tanks and infantry (enemy) would not reach Kew & Richmond for many hours. In fact

even at the worst not for a day or two. By which time the civilians will have dispersed. I consider the chance of an air attack in that locality is not sufficient to stop the pleasures of those who are unable to go further afield to seek relaxation. Should there be signs of an imminent invasion steps should be taken to close Kew and to prevent crowds along the river banks as has been done in areas near E & S coasts.[xiv]

Certain precautions were taken in case of German invasion or a landing by enemy parachutists. During the Blitz members of the Home Guard protected local bridges across the Thames. Colonel A E Redfern said: 'It became a matter of local pride to get on Bridge Guard before the arrival of the regular soldiers, who had motor trucks for their transportation.'[xv]

On the Riverside, pillboxes were built which it was hoped would delay the enemy. Walking along the Thames in December 1941, Stephen Paull found:

> Near the old house [Asgill House] on the banks of the Thames is a machine gun pillbox. Placed to protect the bridge it is in the form of a small brick building with small slits and covered with barbed wire. On the outside are signs: 'Teas, Wines, Eats' − a trick to throw the enemy off guard. Some of these pillboxes are marked 'Ladies and Gentlemen' or some such innocent sign.[xvi]

Although the riverbank seemed safe it was actually quite a dangerous area, for it was covered in shards of glass from windows blown out by air raids. The Whitsuntide bank holiday, at the end of May 1944, brought the crowds to Richmond enjoying the fine late-spring weather. A number of trippers decided to walk barefoot along the towpath in the sunshine, which turned out to be a mistake. Council minutes noted that, as a result, the Heavy Mobile Unit at the Star and Garter Home treated 109 people for cut feet, and the Richmond Royal Hospital treated 27 who required surgical stitching. It was agreed to place warning notices on the lanes leading down to the Thames.[xvii]

As many of the visitors were servicemen and women with their girl and boy friends, it is perhaps not surprising that the riverside became a focus of amorous activities. Bushes along the towpaths were littered with condoms. Roy Featherstone remembers that, 'Ignorant of their significance or use, my sister and I used to collect them in jam jars and took them home, and floated them in the bath. My mother was less than pleased!'[xviii]

[i] http://sas-space.sas.ac.uk/2810/1/Glancy,_Going_to_the_pictures.pdf. The films shown are listed in the local papers.

[ii] *Richmond and Twickenham Times*, 29 May 1943. Patrons could also easily get to the West End cinemas and theatres.

[iii] Knight, Stan, *Memoirs of a Sea Cadet* (typescript), p2.

[iv] Museum of Richmond, *Catalogue for Richmond at War: the Civilian Experience 1939-45* (Museum of Richmond, 1992), p27.

[v] Stephen Paull diary, 21 November 1941.

[vi] *Richmond and Twickenham Times*, 29 May 1943. The Castle remained a notorious pub until the 1970s at least.

[vii] Stephen Paull diary, 4 December 1941.

[viii] Piper Collection, vol 8, p37. Annual Report of Richmond Council for Social Service 1944-5. The party was broadcast on the American Service of the BBC World Service. Mary Buck email to author.

[ix] Museum of Richmond, *Catalogue,* p37.

[x] Hills, R J T, *Phantom was There* (Edward Arnold, 1951), p42.

[xi] Niven, David, *The Moon's a Balloon* (Hamish Hamilton, 1971), p225. There is a thank you letter from Bud Flanagan, who appears to have organised much of the show, in WO 215/13.

[xii] Emergency Committee minutes, 10 September 1940.

[xiii] Mr W B Currell, 28 Cambrian Road, Richmond, 1 August 1940 TNA HO 207/988.

[xiv] Minute from Capt E Hamilton 20 August 1940. TNA HO 207/988.

[xv] Redfern, A E *Reminiscences of the 63rd Surrey (Richmond) Battalion Home Guard* (Richmond, [1946]), p11.

[xvi] Stephen Paull diary, 12 December 1941.

[xvii] Richmond Council minutes, 13 June 1944.

[xviii] Featherstone, Roy, *Memories of Kew in WW2*. See also TNA MEPO 2/6492.

CHAPTER 10 – *Richmond Park*

Richmond Park played a surprisingly significant part in the national war effort, which has now been almost forgotten. It was the largest open space in greater London with good links to central London and across the South East, and so attracted a variety of military units, which were based at various locations in the Park. They included 102 Medical Rehabilitation Unit for-seriously wounded soldiers near Kingston Gate, to anti-aircraft and searchlight batteries by Sheen Gate, as well as the officers' mess of the hush-hush Phantom Regiment in Pembroke Lodge, a 'sterilising pit' used for bleeding explosives from unexploded enemy bombs near Isabella Plantation, and a testing ground used by the Ministry of Home Security to explode German bombs. Lastly it was a training ground for the Home Guard, five members of whom were killed during a training exercise on 17 May 1942, when they accidentally used explosives in making a fire.[i]

According to the Park's historian, Michael Baxter Brown, the war 'disrupted Richmond Park in a greater degree than any other event in its 300 year history'. Routine maintenance work suffered and tree planting was more or less abandoned. Much of the land was turned over to pasture to meet the desperate need for food. As a result the deer were culled in 1943 to as few as 68 fallow and 13 red deer, and they had to share what remained of the grazing with a flock of 350 sheep and 50 head of cattle. However, their condition appeared to improve despite the unusual conditions. Meanwhile Mr D A Rawlence, the Park's Official Bird Watcher, reassured readers of *The Times* in April 1941 that despite the din of anti-aircraft guns at night 'those truly heroic British birds, the herons in Richmond Park, have carried on their nesting and are now feeding their young.'[ii]

Initially the Park remained open to the public, but once the Blitz began in earnest the Park was quickly closed to civilians. Ena Barrett was one of the last to be admitted:

> One day I was watching the Wizard of Oz in the local cinema when the siren sounded and I decided to get home where my mother was alone. Almost immediately there was a series of explosions as one of these German bombers released its load across Richmond Park. After the All Clear, I took the dog into the park and saw several craters at a distance. I didn't investigate, but the park was closed to the public from that day on.[iii]

After the Blitz ended in May 1941 small parts of the Park between Sheen and Richmond gates and near Ham Gate were reopened to the public. However, the Park as a whole remained closed until May 1945. Even then a few areas remained out of bounds, and walkers were warned: 'There are also some mines in the boundary fence of Pembroke Lodge and cottage garden that it has been impracticable to remove.'[iv]

Anti-Aircraft Guns

The military unit in Richmond Park that made the most impact locally was undoubtedly the Ant-Aircraft Battery near Sheen Gate. The guns arrived in the early days of the war as part of the plans to protect London from enemy air attack, although how successful they were is not clear, except in reassuring the population that they were being defended.

An anti-aircraft gun near the Sheen Gate in Richmond Park. The guns reassured local people by their noise, but shot down very few enemy planes.

At first, families and dog-walkers could get close to the guns, which were naturally an attraction to visitors, particularly when they were in action. In August 1940, before the park was closed to visitors, L J Fransella, of

Derby Road, East Sheen complained to the Home Office about the lack of air-raid shelters:

> Yesterday afternoon my wife and young daughter were… on their way home via the East Sheen gates, and passing the battery of anti-aircraft guns when the gunners apparently received the yellow warning and immediately proceeded to action stations (this was about twenty minutes before the sirens were sounded). Many people, including my wife and daughter etc, stopped to watch the activity at the guns. When such instances happen during the day and the Park appears to be crowded, I do think that some warning should be given to the people to make for home without delay, instead of allowing them to stand and watch preparations for action, which may take place at any minute.[v]

Marie Lawrence's diaries are full of references to the noise made by the guns. On 8 September 1940 she wrote that a lone German raider had flown over:

> We rushed downstairs and heard the AA guns pounding away like mad. Terrific noise. We watched from our back windows and saw the shells burst. It was a wonderful sight. They drove him off successfully after about five minutes fire.[vi]

For most of the Blitz the guns were manned by men from 333 Heavy Anti-Aircraft Battery, who arrived from Bude, after training, on 25 September 1940 and finally left for Wanstead on 21 June 1941. During that time the unit war diary suggests they managed to hit just two enemy aircraft. The Luftwaffe bombed the battery on 29 November as part of the big raid on Richmond. The war diary reported:

> A large number of small incendiary bombs dropped around camp and gun site between 1845 and 0030 hours. Two HE of probably 250KG exploded…did some damage to huts, glass and water fittings. Three vehicles on parade ground slightly damaged by splinters. One enemy aircraft fired at 7,000ft and probably hit. Large quantities of smoke were seen in the sky as aircraft flew off. Two casualties from flying glass, both very slight cuts in the head…[vii]

However, the event that stayed in the memory of members of the battery was the surprise visit by Winston Churchill on 10 October. The unit war diary records that he arrived at 2030 hours and spent about 75 minutes with the unit: 'The Prime Minister, Lt Gen Sir Frederick Pyle [sic], Maj Gen Crossman, with other visitors arrive and inspect all instructions on position. They watched unseen target shooting first with VIE [?] and subsequently GL [gun laying].' Sir Frederick Pile was General Officer Commanding Anti-Aircraft Command and Crossman was the Officer Commanding 1 Anti-Aircraft Division.

General Pile wrote in his memoirs that 'I had seen to it that a tin hat had been brought for the Prime Minister but he would not wear it.' During his tour Churchill rejoiced to hear the guns. '"This exhilarates me," declared the Prime Minister bouncing on his heels in the battery operation room. "The sound of these cannon gives me a tremendous feeling."'[viii]

Later in the war the site was closely associated with the AA Command Wireless School (known locally as the 'Radio School'), which was established at All Saints Church in Petersham, in order to improve the accuracy of anti-aircraft guns. 333 HAA Battery was succeeded by 490 HAA Battery, which was the first Anti-Aircraft unit with women as well as men on the establishment acting as range finders and plotters.[*] According to Sir Frederick Pile, 'They became one of the wonders of the world. Women marching, eating, drilling, working with men!' He said that the only real problem had been with the head of the Auxiliary Territorial Service (ATS), who complained 'bitterly that our specially contrived living conditions [at the site] were "disgraceful".'

When Churchill visited this unit in the summer of 1941, he 'seemed most impressed: he repeated several times that it was a remarkable and satisfactory innovation.' Whether he met Violet Akehurst is not known. She became the youngest female casualty of the war. She was stationed in Richmond Park during the summer of 1941 but died of pneumococcal meningitis at Bath Military Hospital on 24 November 1941 aged just sixteen.[ix]

The Starfish Decoy

Richmond Park was also used as a location for a decoy against enemy air attacks. During the war nearly 800 such decoys were built across the United Kingdom. Their intention was to draw Luftwaffe bombers away from military targets and centres of civilian population. The most advanced type was the Starfish (from the abbreviation for Special Fire),

---

[*] For more about this research station see Lee, J M, *Petersham: radar and operational research* (RLHS, 2011), particularly p17 on the mixed unit.

one of which was built near White Lodge. The Starfish decoy in the Park was one of six built in the London area. On 6 December 1940, the Chiefs of Staff agreed that such a facility be constructed as a matter of some urgency because 'a major decoy fire within reasonable distance of the centre [of London] is necessary. The only suitable site for this purpose is Richmond Park....'[x]

By day these sites resembled nothing more than chicken sheds, but they were equipped with specially-designed boilers and fire baskets which, when ignited at night, resembled exploding bombs, burning incendiaries and buildings on fire. The dramatic effects could be made to last a number of hours. Trevor Denniff who worked on these decoys later wrote:

> Pairs of one thousand gallon galvanised tanks were positioned on top of 20 foot high towers, one filled with water and the other with diesel or paraffin. Under each tank a simple control system like a WC flush released the liquids down pipes into 15-foot heavy cast iron troughs filled with coal or coke over a bed of fire lighter materials. Electrically wired flash bang detonators assured ignition by a switch in the dugout. The idea was that the coal would be lit when enemy bombers were in the area at night and after the cast iron trough was good and hot the diesel was released. This boiled and the vapours ignited. The water was then released onto the burning oil causing a virtual explosion of fire and steam. It was all very impressive.[xi]

It is hard to know how effective such decoys were. Apparently they were easily spotted from the air. A Luftwaffe prisoner of war told his interrogators in early 1941 that 'London was said to have four [decoy] zones...the second Richmond Park...' Perhaps it didn't matter. Even if they had been told about Starfish, inexperienced or harassed aircrew at night could easily mistake the realistic decoys for the real thing.

The decoys' historian Colin Dobinson believes that they prevented one in twenty bombs falling on their intended targets. The success of the one in Richmond Park may be seen by the large number of bombs that fell in the south-west quadrant of the Park rather than on the neighbouring suburbs.[xii]

Phantom

Of all the military units operating in and around Richmond the most exotic was probably the Phantom Regiment, officially the GHQ Liaison Regiment. Mysterious even today, the unit was meant to be the eyes and ears of the commanders in the field, reporting directly to them and by-passing the usual means of communication. Its first commander, the charismatic Lt Col 'Hoppy' Hopkinson, explained his troops' role:

> Their job is to find information in the 'blind spots' and transmit it direct back to GHQ. They are left to use what means they like to obtain the information. Either by direct observation or by liaison with various HQ up to Corps but the main principle being that any information is transmitted by code direct to the Commander in Chief.[xiii]

The unit was set up in the aftermath of the fall of France and would have played an important part had Britain been invaded in 1940. Richmond was an ideal location close to the military authorities in London, with good road links. The regimental headquarters was in the semi-derelict Richmond Hill Hotel, with its large dining room and kitchens. The basement housed the workshops repairing the unit's vehicles and wirelesses. Officers were housed in Pembroke Lodge while the men were billeted in private houses locally. However the Lodge was not safe from German bombs. Phantom's quartermaster, Major R J T Hills, recalled:

> Over four hundred bombs fell in the Park and Hoppy liked to think we ourselves were the attraction to the Luftwaffe. Certainly one bomb destroyed a hideous blue stone peacock in our garden. The windows were oftener out than in. Hoppy considered flinging oneself to the carpet on such occasions as 'not quite the thing'. Two officers out of thirty gained a quite unfair reputation for gallantry one evening as being the only two off the floor when the CO came in. Actually diving inwards on the same settee, they had met in mid-air and stunned each other.[xiv]

And at least once the Lodge was struck by lightning:

> A violent thunderstorm caused considerable confusion at RHQ: a number of telephone lines notably the direct line to the STARFISH [decoy] site in Richmond Park were put out of action; the telephone exchange, in common with a considerable part of the rest of RHQ billets was flooded, resulting in further dislocation of telephonic communications, which were not improved by the collapse of the roof on the exchange operator's head.[xv]

Basic training took place in Richmond Park, but squadrons were always being sent on training missions across southern England or later on operational missions overseas. It was intensive and extensive work with much emphasis on being able to effectively use the rather cumbersome and temperamental wireless sets of the period.

By 1942 increasing numbers of Phantom units were serving overseas, so numbers locally began to decline. Peter Horrocks arrived in the summer of 1944 during Phantom's declining days:

> I was summoned to that regiment's headquarters, then in Richmond Park, Surrey, for assessment and training in that force's particular role. The main requirements seemed to be: above average ability to drive, reasonable competence with radio communications (I never really mastered the Morse code!), ability to write concise messages, mastery of their cipher system.[xvi]

Horrocks was one of the last officers to pass through the unit. Eventually only the Regimental Headquarters and the Training and Holding Unit – preparing men for active service – were left, and Richmond Park could begin to return to a more peaceable role.

[i] Brown, Michael Baxter, *Richmond Park: the history of a royal deer park* (Robert Hale, 1985), p194. Reports of tests on bombs and mines can be found in series HO 196 at The National Archives.

[ii] *Manchester Guardian*, 25 May 1942, *The Times*, 25 May 1942.
Brown, p194. *The Times*, 18 April 1941. For the Park in wartime also see Porter, Frank, *Barnes and Mortlake at War* (Barnes and Mortlake LHS, forthcoming).

[iii] Ena Barrett contribution to the BBC People's War Project www.bbc.co.uk/history/ww2peopleswar/stories/54/a4452554.shtml.

[iv] *The Times*, 5 July 1941. *Thames Valley Times*, 2 May 1945.

[v] L J Fransella, 14 Derby Gate, London SW14 to the Minister for Home Security, 14 August 1940. TNA HO 207/988.

[vi] For a detailed discussion of Britain's anti-aircraft defences and their effectiveness see Dobinson, Colin, *AA Command: British Anti-Aircraft Defences of World War II* (Methuen, 2001). The co-ordinates of Richmond's battery (code named ZS20) are TQ204743. Marie Lawrence diary entry for 8 September 1940. There was also another battery in Richmond Park (ZS19) near Robin Hood Gate.

[vii] Unit war diary TNA WO 166/2602, 29 November 1940. The other plane was hit on 6 November 1940.

[viii] WO 166/2602 10 October 1940. Pile, Frederick, *Ack Ack: Britain's defence against air attack during the Second World War* (Harrap, 1949), p169. See also Dobinson, *AA Command*, p265.

[ix] Pile, pp191-192, 222. Thanks to Kevin Regan for the information about Violet Akehurst. She is buried in Battle.

[x] TNA CAB 80/24 memorandum no 1020. The grid reference is TQ204730. See also Dobinson, Colin, *Fields of Deception: Britain's bombing decoys of the Second World War* (Methuen, 2000), pp89-95. There are unsubstantiated reports that the decoy moved to Hampstead Heath during 1942.

[xi] Quoted in webpage on the St Margaret's Community Website www.stmgrts.org.uk/archives/2012/05/richmond_park_starfish_bombing_decoy_sf8a.html.

[xii] TNA HO 198/239. Dobinson, *Fields* Pix.

[xiii] TNA WO 215/13 letter of 17 November 1941. In practice as one of its officers, David Niven, later wrote, the message would normally be 'that the situation was unclear because the place was full of Germans.' David Niven, *The Moon's a Balloon* (Hamish Hamilton, 1971), p220.

[xiv] Hills, R J T, *Phantom was There* (Edward Arnold, 1951), p38. Much of this section is based on this book, which remains the only real account of GHQ Liaison Regiment.

[xv] Regimental war diary, 4 July 1942 WO 215/16.

[xvi] Peter Horrocks contribution to the BBC People's War Project www.bbc.co.uk/history/ww2peopleswar/stories/13/a3830113.shtml.

CHAPTER 11 – *Aftermath*

The end of the war found Richmond battered but defiantly unbowed. Most residents would have agreed with the *Richmond Herald* that 'life was not easy, yet the people were wonderfully cheery and the life of the town went on.'[i]

On VE-Day, 8 May 1945, which celebrated final victory over the Nazis, there were tremendous festivities in Richmond. (VJ-Day, in August, celebrating victory over Japan, would be a quieter affair.)

The VE-Day party held in Manor Grove

The *Richmond and Twickenham Times* reported:
> During the morning and afternoon of the great day Richmond enjoyed comparative quiet. There was a continual throng moving through the town, however, and the riverside was crowded with leisured strollers and hundreds of jubilant children…. When dusk began to fall, Richmond let herself go. People poured from the riverside and surrounding districts joining with the carefree throngs parading Hill Street and George Street. Groups with coloured hats and shining faces danced and laughed themselves to

exhaustion outside The Ship in King Street, while in other parts of the town men and women sang sentimental songs or with changing mood danced jigs. Many servicemen were with Richmond's victory crowds and at the railway station a sailor, looking much the worse for wear, but tremendously happy, was wandering blissfully along draped in a Union Jack... Silence did not reign until the early hours of the morning.[ii]

The Revd Harold Gray, Vicar of St Mary Magdalene, had a rather different experience:

After days of almost hourly expectation of the great news, we were told on Monday evening... The nation's thankfulness found spontaneous expression in the great thanksgiving services held everywhere. Our own Parish Church was packed for the evening service, which the Borough Council had asked might be made the civic expression of our gratitude and which the Mayor and Corporation attended in their robes.[*][iii]

However, for most people in Richmond the psychological end of the war was on 2 July when Winston Churchill paid a whistle-stop visit. As part of the Conservative General Election campaign Churchill made a triumphant procession through south west London. The event had been well publicised and tens of thousands turned out to cheer the Prime Minister. At 5.45pm he was due to arrive on Richmond Green, where he was to speak on behalf of the Conservative candidate George Harvie-Watt, Churchill's Principal Parliamentary Secretary.

He arrived in Richmond along the Lower Mortlake Road. *The Times* reporter wrote that the Prime Minister was smiling as 'he smoked his cigar and alternatively gave the V sign or waved his hat.'[iv]

Marie Lawrence noted: 'People were thronging everywhere to see Winnie. I ... met Mrs Humphreys who was waiting for Churchill. Just at that moment came the outriders, then the mounted police, then a long open car and standing in the middle making the V sign Churchill. The crowd went wild and shouted and cheered.'[v]

---

[*] Otherwise, few citizens of Richmond or anywhere else spent VE-Day in church. The nation seems to have taken to the streets rather than the pews.

The Prime Minister drove to Richmond Green, which was full of thousands of his supporters. There is a short clip of film at Richmond Local Studies Library showing the PM's arrival. Churchill is waving his hat. Standing on the running board of the car are two Special Branch officers looking for all the world like American gangsters.

Winston Churchill driving through Richmond to the public meeting held on the Green on 2 July 1945

The Times reported:

> Churchill's car stopped under some trees and here he made a long speech… Mr Churchill's voice amplified by loud speakers was resonant and was clearly heard. 'Can you hear me?' he asked at the beginning. Then 'Are we downhearted?' When the cheers in response died away he said amid laughter 'I only do this to test the microphone.' He then spoke in support of Harvie-Watt outlining his policies to rebuild post-war Britain.

As Mr Churchill drove away, 'the people ran across the Green to give him a parting cheer.' *The Times* reporter concluded: 'In a short time only a few people were left to listen to an address in an obscure corner of the cricket field on behalf of the Liberal candidate.'

Harvie-Watt held Richmond comfortably, although his majority was much reduced.

Planning for the Future

Richmond in 1945 was shabby and scarred by six years of war. As early as November 1941 Lt Paull had noted:

> A stranger is reminded of the war only by the scars which are visible in many parts of the town. Here one finds a house completely demolished, there a house partly wrecked. On our street a great many windows are broken and many houses are undergoing minor repairs.[vi]

Although the town had suffered less than many other places thousands of buildings had been damaged in the raids, and shops were bare. However, Richmond's citizens were healthier than they had ever been and if their diet was rationed and very dull this was not reflected in the mortality figures. The borough's Temporary Medical Officer of Health, John Dancy, wrote in his report for 1945, 'Despite the War the physical health of the civil population has suffered remarkably little.' The death rate was slightly above the pre-war level, but births were significantly higher, particularly among children born out of wedlock: 'The illegitimacy [rate] still stands disquietingly high.' This was a side effect of the rash of wartime liaisons between servicemen and local women, and was repeated nationwide.[vii]

In the later half of the war, local councils prepared plans to rebuild and revitalise their areas. In particular the London County Council commissioned Professor Sir Leslie Abercrombie to draw up a plan to take advantage of the Blitz and rebuild the metropolis, which was published in 1944 to great acclaim. A few months later in March 1945 Richmond Council published *Towards a Plan for Richmond*, its blueprint for the future of the town. The Plan itself is rather limited. Its authors J W Todd, the Borough Engineer, and his assistant Stanley Weddle were clearly constrained by the peculiar geography of the borough with its large number of open spaces and historic buildings, as well as the natural conservatism of the Council itself – it only gave the plan a rather lukewarm blessing, rather than its approval. The main proposal was to build a wide plaza through central Richmond from St Mary's Church to a new civic centre on the site of the town hall. Traffic would be diverted from the town, by the construction of a new by-pass. Modern schools would be built and, controversially, the plan proposed that the population of the borough be limited to 40,000.[viii]

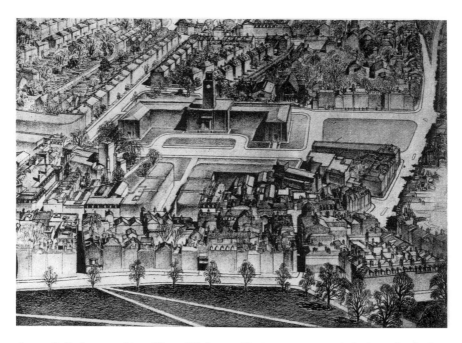

An artist's impression of how Richmond's town centre might have looked had it been rebuilt as planned

The parish magazine welcomed the proposal:

> A most ambitious scheme involving the demolition of the cinema and shops opposite Richmond Bridge and also the Bus terminus and other places to create a great civic centre. As you come over Richmond Bridge you would then come to a fine square, with a view of the Parish Church on one side, the lovely old houses in Ormond Road on the other and the Town Hall and Civic Centre in the middle.[ix]

The publication was accompanied by an exhibition at the Town Hall where people could come to look at the proposals. Perhaps fortunately, a lack of resources in the immediate post-war period meant that the Plan largely came to nothing.[x]

The town slowly recovered from the war, although there were bombsites until well into the 1950s, and in the early 1990s trees in Kew Road still showed signs of the painted white rings that increased their visibility during the blackout. For years it was not uncommon for gardeners to uncover small caches of ammunition or shrapnel.

As the threat of air raids had declined, all the shelters had begun to be neglected. Anderson shelters became useful greenhouses and the public shelters were mostly closed. In March 1945 Richmond Council discussed the state of the shelter on Richmond Green and agreed to repair the fences surrounding it, supply new electric light cables, and fit the gates with opening and closing devices to stop people getting inside, but after the war came to an end the shelters were quickly dismantled.[xi] If requested, the Council would remove Anderson shelters, but one or two still survive.[xii]

The symbol of Richmond's recovery was the restoration of the Town Hall on Hill Street, although many changes were made to improve conditions for the councillors during the rebuilding. It was opened by Queen Elizabeth the Queen Mother on 16 December 1952, almost twelve years to the day since the building was severely damaged in the Blitz, and sixteen years since planning for war began.[xiii]

Over time the physical and, one likes to think, the psychological scars have healed. Almost nothing physically survives as a reminder. Now only the old have any clear memories of the war, which to their great-grand children must seem like ancient history, to be mentioned in the same breath as Henry VIII or the Romans.

The people of the town, like British citizens everywhere, endured hardships, grumbled, yet were remarkably united and determined to beat Hitler and Fascism. To them we must be grateful. The alternative would have been unthinkable.

---

[i]   *Richmond Herald,* 8 December 1945.
[ii]   *Richmond and Twickenham Times*, 12 May 1945, p7.
[iii]   *St Mary Magdalene Parish Magazine*, May 1945.
[iv]   *The Times*, 3 July 1945.
[v]   Marie Lawrence's diary 2 July 1945.
[vi]   Stephen Paull papers, diary entry 19 November 1941, Imperial War Museum.
[vii]   Medical Officer of Health Annual Report 1945, pp8-9.
[viii] Richmond Council minutes, 13 March 1945.
[ix]   *St Mary Magdalene Parish Magazine*, April 1945.
[x]   Todd. J W, and Weddle S, *Towards a plan for Richmond* (Richmond Borough Council, 1945).
[xi]   Richmond Council minutes, 13 March 1945.
[xii]   Museum of Richmond, *Catalogue for Richmond at War: the Civilian Experience 1939-45* (Museum of Richmond, 1992).
[xiii] See Local History Note at www.richmond.gov.uk/local_history_old_town_hall.pdf for more about the restoration.

Appendix 1   Bombs and Casualties

These figures were compiled by Richmond Council after the war and, unless otherwise indicated, are for the whole borough, not just the town. Although at first sight they seem dramatic, in fact they show how unscathed the borough actually was. Only a quarter of one per cent of the town's population were killed in raids and, very roughly, two per cent of its housing stock was totally destroyed by bombs.[*]

Air raids

The first raid took place on 9 September 1940, when at 4am High Explosive bombs fell on 35 Mount Ararat Road, and 36 Marchmont Road. The worst night was 29 November 1940 when 35 bombs fell on the town.

Raids took place on the following dates. The major raids have been underlined.

1940

September 9, 14, 16, 20, 24, 26, 29, 30

October 1, 4, 7, 9, 10, 13, 14, 15, 16, 19, 28

November 1, 7, 8, 9, 12, 16, 17, 18, 19, 29, 30

December 1, 9

1941

April 16

1942 none

1943 November 8

1944 February 26

June 19, 26, 27; July 23; August 20, 23, 27; September 20;

October 25 — all V1s. September 12 – V2

1945 none

March 15 V2

In addition there were 1,217 alerts (that is when the air-raid sirens sounded). The first was shortly after the declaration of war on 3 September 1939, the final one was on 29 March 1945. In total they lasted 88 days 14 hours 28 minutes; the longest alert was on 11 November 1940, of 14 hours 14 minutes and the shortest was on 14 July 1944, which lasted just two minutes.

---

[*] The figures used here are largely taken from a report in the *Richmond Herald*, 8 December 1945, and a bomb census prepared by the Council in 1946.

Bombs dropped

Excluding Richmond Park, the following bombs were dropped on Richmond: 211 High Explosive bombs (of which 37 were unexploded); seven phosphorus bombs (two unexploded).

Two land mines, on Courtlands and Peldon Avenue, on 20 September 1940; and one, which was unexploded, on Sandycombe Road, Kew, on 26 September 1940.

Thirteen oil bombs; ten flying bombs (V1) and one V2 rocket in addition to thousands of incendiaries.

Within Richmond Park, 297 high explosive bombs fell, as well as four flying bombs (V1) and one V2 rocket.

Casualties

97 men women and children were killed during the raids, including five fire-watchers. In addition, 397 people were injured, of whom 133 were treated by first-aid posts and mobile units. Among the injured were fourteen air-raid wardens.

Housing

297 houses had to be demolished as the result of the air raids. In addition 272 properties were severely damaged. In addition 11,523 premises were damaged, some more than once.

762 people were rendered homeless and were permanently rehoused mainly within the borough. In addition, ten half-way houses were requisitioned and adapted for occupation by 149 people, and another fifteen were requisitioned for foreign (mainly Belgian) war refugees.

Appendix 2   Public shelters in Richmond, Dec 1941

These are shelters that were available in Richmond town only. They were either open at the time the list was compiled or had been used at some stage during the War, and subsequently were closed. Additional shelters were of course also provided elsewhere in the borough.

Location	Open or closed	Type of shelter	No of bunks	No of people
Old Deer Park	Open	Trench	231	256
2 & 4 Pagoda Avenue	Open	Basement	9	50
137 & 139 Kew Road	Open	Basement	45	65
Raleigh Gardens	Closed	Trench	75	87
Lower Mortlake Road Rec. Ground	Closed	Trench	75	87
Lower Mortlake Road School	Open	School	0	110
West Sheen Vale	Open	Trench	42	67
Grena Road	Open	Trench	0	50
Manor Road allotments	Closed	Surface	48	48
Richmond Green	Open	Trench	501	601
Water Lane	Open	Surface	33	33
Halford Road	Open	Surface	18	30
Richmond Bridge arches	Closed	Arches	255	345
St Elizabeth's Church	Open	Basement	60	72
Vineyard School	Open	School	0	255
Eton Lodge	Open	School	0	75
Paradise Road	Open	School	0	40
Town Hall	Closed	Basement	48	108
Richmond Station	Closed	Arches	60	63
Park Lane	Open	School	0	185
1 Spring Terrace	Closed	Basement	27	39
6 Spring Terrace	Closed	Basement	21	31
Station arches	Open	Arches	60	63
118-129 Sheen Road	Open	Basement	150	200
68 King's Road	Open	School	0	50
27 King's Road	Closed	Surface	27	27

Pest House Common, Grove Road	Closed	Trench	18	43
Black House	Open	Trench	21	46
Grove Road Recreation Ground	Closed	Trench	21	37
Onslow Road	Open	Surface	18	30
76 Mt Ararat Road	Closed	Basement	21	39
96 Church Road	Open	Basement	18	24
98 Church Road	Open	Basement	24	28
100 Church Road	Open	Basement	24	28
102 Church Road	Open	Basement	24	28
Terrace Field (Upper)	Closed	Trench	21	38
Terrace Field (Lower)	Closed	Trench	15	32
Terrace Field (arches)	Open	Arches	0	80
Buccleuch tunnels	Open	Trench	0	50
Richmond Park Gates	Open	Trench	15	32
Friars Stile Road	Open	Basement	0	130
Chisholm Road	Closed	Surface	0	130
Bute House tunnel	Open	Trench	24	47

Source TNA HO 207/988

Appendix 3   Sources

Bibliography

This is a list of books and pamphlets consulted during the writing of this book. Copies of the purely local material should be available at the Local Studies Library and Archive at the Old Town Hall, Whittaker Avenue, Richmond.

Barnfield, Paul, *When the Bombs Fell: Twickenham, Teddington and the Hamptons under Aerial Bombardment during the Second World War* (Borough of Twickenham Local History Society, 2001)

Blomfield, David, and May, Christopher, *Kew at War* (Richmond Local History Society, 2009)

Brown, Michael Baxter, *Richmond Park: the history of a royal deer park* (Robert Hale, 1985)

Chave, Leonard, & Lee, J M, *Ham and Petersham in Wartime* (Richmond Local History Society, 2013)

Dobinson, Colin, *AA Command: British Anti-Aircraft Defences of World War II* (Methuen, 2001)

Dobinson, Colin, *Fields of Deception: Britain's bombing decoys of the Second World War* (Methuen, 2000)

Gardiner, Juliet, *The Blitz: the British under attack* (Harper Press, 2010)

Hills, R J T, *Phantom was There* (Edward Arnold, 1951)

Lee, J M, *Petersham: radar and operational research* (Richmond Local History Society, 2011)

Museum of Richmond, *Catalogue for Richmond at War: the Civilian Experience 1939-45* (Museum of Richmond, 1993)

Niven, David, *The Moon's a Balloon* (Hamish Hamilton, 1971)

Pawle, Gerald, *The Secret War 1939-1945* (Harrap, 1955)

Pile, Frederick, *Ack Ack: Britain's defence against air attack during the Second World War* (Harrap, 1949)

Porter, Frank, *Barnes and Mortlake at War* (Barnes and Mortlake History Society, forthcoming)

Redfern, A E, *Reminiscences of the 63rd Surrey (Richmond) Battalion Home Guard* (Richmond, 1946)

Scudamore, Margaret, *The Richmond and East Sheen County School for Girls: a record 1861-1947* (Richmond, 1947)

Websites
The Richmond Local History Society's own website contains a number of posts which may be of interest www.richmondhistory.org.uk
The St Margaret's Community website has several interesting pages relating to the War in Richmond www.stmgrts.org.uk
A fascinating interactive map showing where the bombs fell on Greater London between 7 October 1940 and 6 June 1941 is at www.bombsight.org. Unfortunately it is not entirely accurate.

Newspapers
Richmond Herald, Richmond and Twickenham Times, Thames Valley Times – particularly the files of clippings maintained by the Local Studies Library. Of the national papers *The Times* was particularly useful.

Archives
We are blessed in having an excellent Local Studies Library at the top of Richmond Old Town Hall, which has many records pertaining to the Second World War. Of particular importance is Marie Lawrence's diary, a detailed account of the life and experiences of a young woman during the period, and the school log books for the County Boys and Girls secondary schools which provide a unique perspective on the Blitz. There are also several scrapbooks of press cuttings including the Piper Collection which was compiled by William Piper, the borough librarian during the war.

Local historians in Richmond are uniquely lucky in having the resources of The National Archives in Kew on our doorstep. There is a reasonable amount about the history of the town during the War, particularly in the Home Office and War Office collections. References to individual files used are given in the endnotes (prefaced with the abbreviation TNA).

In Woking, the Surrey History Centre has records of the Surrey County Council, the Richmond Royal Hospital, some school logs and court and church records.

The Imperial War Museum has the diary of the American signals technician Lt Stephen Paull, who was based in the town from late 1941.

The Hearsum Collection at Pembroke Lodge has some material about Phantom, and David Catford's notes on Richmond Park, for a history of Barnes and Mortlake in WW2, which unfortunately was never published.

Details of the civilian casualties are on the Commonwealth War Graves Commission website www.cwgc.org. A roll of honour with the names inscribed of those civilians who were killed in the Borough is displayed at the Old Town Hall.

Oral history and autobiographies

Alette Anderson conducted interviews with six Richmond residents who remembered the War: Leoni Burke, Rachel Dickson, Jack Tuckwell, Gwen and Betty Watts, and Nigel Williamson.

Felix O'Kelly supplied a transcript of an interview he did with his grandmother Aleksandra Parry-Jones, and Stan Knight and Roy Featherstone supplied short autobiographies.

Mary Buck, Mike Evans, Roy Featherstone, Walter D'Hondt and Stan Knight wrote to me with their memories of their wartime childhoods. Elsie Erlebach let me have some of her papers. In addition the BBC People's War website – www.bbc.co.uk/history/ww2peopleswar – contains a number of stories submitted by people who lived in the area. Material is used by permission of the BBC, but copyright resides with the contributors.

Museums

The excellent Museum of Richmond at the Old Town Hall has several interesting display cases devoted to the Second World War. Admission is free. Details at www.museumofrichmond.com.

ACKNOWLEDGMENTS

This book has received help from an unusually large number of people:

Alette Anderson conducted a number of oral history interviews. Felix O'Kelly added the transcript of the interview he conducted with his grandmother, Aleksandra Parry-Jones. David Blomfield commissioned the book for the Richmond Local History Society, and saw it through the press. Judith Church proof-read the text. Robert Smith promoted the book on the Society's website.

At the Richmond Local Studies Library Jane Baxter, Felix Lancaster and their colleagues offered advice, dug out documents, and pointed me in the right direction for material on the open shelves.

Sue Barber and Natascha Wintersinger of the Museum of Richmond agreed to put on the accompanying exhibition, partly funded by Richmond's Civic Pride fund.

Robert Wood and Daniel Hearsum of the Hearsum Collection at Pembroke Lodge in Richmond Park provided access to their archives and some illustrations. Stephen Harrison gave us permission to use the painting by his mother Mary Kent Harrison, 'Richmond Hill on VE Day'.

Laurence Bain shared his research about the fate of the railings on Richmond Green, and Bob Clarke provided a copy of the Roll of Honour for All Saints Congregational Church in East Sheen, Kevin Regan told me about Violet Akehurst.

Finally Antony Roberts Estate Agents generously gave £250 towards the research for the book.

The author adds that any errors and omissions are his alone.

Index